T0127153

8 WAYS TO
DeClutter
YOUR BRAIN

8 WAYS TO *DeClutter* YOUR BRAIN

Theresa Puskar

Published 2020 by Gildan Media LLC
aka G&D Media
www.GandDmedia.com

8 WAYS TO DECLUTTER YOUR BRAIN. Copyright ©2020 by Theresa Puskar. All rights reserved.

No part of this book may be used, reproduced or transmitted in any manner whatsoever, by any means (electronic, photocopying, recording, or otherwise), without the prior written permission of the author, except in the case of brief quotations embodied in critical articles and reviews. No liability is assumed with respect to the use of the information contained within. Although every precaution has been taken, the author and publisher assume no liability for errors or omissions. Neither is any liability assumed for damages resulting from the use of the information contained herein.

Front cover design by David Rheinhardt of Pyrographx

Interior design by Meghan Day Healey of Story Horse, LLC

Library of Congress Cataloging-in-Publication Data is available upon request

ISBN: 978-1-7225-0266-9

10   9   8   7   6   5   4   3   2   1

Contents

Acknowledgments

There are many people who helped to make this book possible.

• My darling daughter, Bernadette, who brings such light and love into my life. Thank you for being you and especially for your design insights and suggestions.

• My dear friend Susan Pluto, who, above and beyond providing me huge emotional support, was also my second set of eyes. Your editing prowess saved me, girlfriend!

• My thoughtful wasband (ex-husband), Paul, for being my third set of eyes. Your candor and insights on the contents of this book have been wonderfully astute!

• My Oneness family both in Chicago and in India.

• My three Score marketeers, Chuck, Bruce and Gerry. You have lifted my spirits when I most needed it. You gave outstanding advice, but more than that, you gave me hope when I was feeling down.

• My sweet friend, Rebecca. You are such an inspiration as a mother, as a writer, and as a dear friend.

• Mary Anne Carswell, my first extraordinary therapist many decades ago in Toronto.

• My parents, Gerri and Paul, and my three sisters, Laura, Kathy and Carolyn . . . and the rest of my wonderful family back home in Canada.

I am so grateful that you are in my life. I truly am blessed.

In this book, I have mentioned many other individuals who have supported me on my journey towards self-acceptance and higher consciousness. You are my human angels, and I deeply appreciate you: Sri Amma Bhagavan; Dr. David Hawkins; Malcolm Gladwell; Jackie Mellen; Frank Mallinder; Thomas Leonard; Sonia Choquette; Wayne Dyer; Marianne Williamson; Louise Hay; Duane and Catherine O'Kane; Debbie Ford; Byron Katie; Eckhardt Tolle; Luanne Oakes; Jarod Kintz; Shannon Alder; Omari Martin; Christiane Northrup, MD; Esther Hicks; Bharat Kilra; Kasia Suzmali; Sheila Zangar; Theresa Cordova; Ron Roth; Oprah Winfrey

Many thanks to each and every one of you.

My mission with this book is to awaken you to the realization that you have been choosing fear and that you can reroute your personal journey from fear to love, experiencing greater synchronicity, ease, and joy in your life.

Foreword

How do you handle a nightmare?

2019 was the worst year of my life. Death. Divorce. Illness. Sadness. Anguish. It piled up to such an extent that I wanted to exit life, stage left. But then a family member attempted suicide, and I felt the harrowing impact of his decision. I knew the only way out of my year-long predicament was through it.

It's now 2020 and life still rocks my boat, only now I have more tools to handle the queasiness. Many of those tools are right in this book.

Learning how to "declutter" the mind is probably the most useful skill you can acquire to have a happy, successful life. After all, whether you believe you are failing, or succeeding, is all only a difference of a thought. It all happens in your mind. It's all under your inner control.

This book will help you handle life, no matter what gets thrown at you or attracted to you. I personally know Theresa and endorse her and her work. She's walked on the hot coals of life and she's transcended the mediocracy of the mundane. She's learned how to declutter the mind, and now she wants to share this wisdom with you.

How do you handle the nightmares of life?

By awakening.

This book reveals how.

Turn the pages and . . . Expect Miracles.

Dr Joe Vitale
Author of too many books to list here
www.MrFire.com

Prologue

An Accidental Awakening?

"Oh, God. No!" Foot slamming against an unresponsive brake pedal. Slamming again, and again. Slipping, sliding, rolling, falling—no way to control. Terror blasts through every cell of my being. I feel helpless. I *am* helpless!

Time seemed to stand still as I hurled through the air in my speeding car—a real-life roller coaster gone awry. A puny, crap box of failed safety ratings, sliding out of control on merciless black ice—flying through the air, rolling along the grassy median, again and again, and ultimately tearing into my skin during a full-throttle Canadian blizzard. Out of control. *"Dear God, help! I've lost control."* Then darkness.

Forty minutes later, when I regained consciousness, I felt deeply, very deeply. The first thing I did was mutter the name *Kevin*. I experienced his love in a profound way. It was palpable and comforting. I later discovered that he was the paramedic who tended to me in the ambulance. His compassion was deep and real, and I will never forget it. It consoled and reassured me as I struggled to return to consciousness.

Soon after arriving in the ER, I was overcome with extreme pain as I felt the hard, cold stretcher press against my aching back. I felt slight relief when the thoughtful attendants continuously placed and replaced heated blankets over my shocked, shake-and-bake body for what seemed to be hours.

I remember the attending doctor. He was deliciously handsome, and I felt butterflies in my turbulent and traumatized stomach as he diagnosed my condition. He asked me if I knew what day it was. I couldn't recall, but before I fully realized my whereabouts, I uttered, "I'm pregnant. I think I'm pregnant. Please don't give me any drugs."

He responded, "Do you know what day it is?"

I had no idea.

"Do you know how pregnant you are?"

"Three months. I think I'm about three months along."

Soon after his preliminary examination, I remember saying, "Please call my mother." He asked me if I remembered her phone number, and I recited the number without hesitation. Despite the multitude of bandages that were wrapped around my bloodied head, with my quick response, he knew that I was not suffering severe brain damage. Several caregivers examined my face and head, and I could sense their concern. I assumed that I had survived a massive, ugly injury to my face. I had imagined it as scarred and deformed.

Throughout this ordeal, I was having a constant inner dialogue with my creator. I remember thinking, "Hey, God. If I'm deformed, so be it. I've been an actress for over twenty years, when my looks were so important. But I'm going to be a mother now, and if this child survives this, I don't need a pretty face. I'll be just fine."

ER Doctor Delish eventually called my mother, and after I spoke with her, he informed me that his hospital did not have the resources to properly tend to my condition. Soon after, another ambulance whisked me away to a larger hospital. For several hours, I was in a heightened state of alertness. I remember every detail in vivid, vibrant color. I could feel the love and concern of those who cared for me in a very deep way. It was as if I were seeing with their hearts. My eyes were closed, and my head bandaged, but when I heard footsteps, I could recognize who was approaching by the sound and speed of their pace. "That's Mom . . . Hi, husband . . . Dad, that's you, isn't it?"

As it turned out, I fractured the C7 and T1 vertebrae of my spine. I also had a compression fracture, and the frontal lobe of my head had been pierced by a sharp object. It tore most of my scalp off, leaving a flap of skin still adhering to the back of my head. It was like an opened can of soup, with a tiny piece of the lid that had not succumbed to the sharp, steel blade of the can opener. But my can opener was a 3,000-pound automobile.

It required over 500 stitches to reattach my scalp, and I went through the five-hour stitching procedure without even a local anesthetic. I remember the doctor mumbling, "Ouch, ouch, ouch," as he stitched.

But I was determined. I had a new life growing within me, and I wanted her to suffer no more than she already had with the car accident (although I don't like to refer to it as an accident, because I don't believe there was anything accidental about it).

In retrospect, it is crystal-clear to me that I completely surrendered to the moment. The fear that had overwhelmed me as I slammed the brakes and clung to the wheel of my car had melted away. My ego was nonexistent, and I was 100 percent present. I didn't care if I was deformed. I was at one with those who cared for me, experiencing their open hearts as if they were mine. I was not lost in angst about yesteryears or panicking about the worries of tomorrow. I was physically and emotionally present and totally aware. Despite the terror and trauma that I had undergone, I knew that all was well and I was fine.

Soon after the shock of the trauma wore out, my ego returned in full force. "A scar? I have a two-inch scar upon my forehead? Oh, no. Will my hair cover it? Will it grow less ugly and obvious?" But for a short and potent period of time, I relinquished control (or should I say that control was relinquished for me?), and I was in an altered state of consciousness.

Was it the state of shock I was in? Was it where I had journeyed to during the forty minutes that I was unconscious? I will never know, but I do know that ever since this "accidental" awakening, I've been trying to return there once again!

Be Careful about What You Wish For:
You Just Might Receive It . . . in Droves!

As I sat in bed, recuperating at my parents' home in Canada, I pondered the pickle I had gotten myself into. I realized that, prior to my automotive awakening, I had been telling myself, "I've got to take the time out of my busy schedule to get quiet and meditate." After years of producing audio programs with *New York Times* best-selling experts on success, I had no doubt that taking the time to do so would declutter my crazy, nonstop brain and shift my life in profound and powerful ways.

I'd also been thinking, "I want to really know in my heart of hearts that my value is not in what I do. I want to fully embrace the fact that I am enough simply by being here on this earth. I don't need to produce anything or please anyone."

After the incident, I was bedridden for three months. I had plenty of time to explore silence in an unproductive state of simply "being." Be careful what you wish for, especially if you are a powerful manifester!

This episode took me through a rebirth of sorts. The presence and quieting of the brain that I experienced during the first several hours at the hospital introduced me to a different state of being.

Let me be clear, however, that you don't have to undergo such drama and trauma to declutter your brain. In fact, since the incident, I make a point of requesting that future responses to my intentions be delivered to me in less traumatic, gentler, and easier-to-open packages than the crash.

Did the car awakening work? Was it effective? Yes and no. I sat in quiet for three months, and I learned to sit in solitude and gratitude without being able to identify myself through my work. Did it last? No. The experience had opened a portal, but it was a small door into a vast world of transformation that has since taken me on a fascinating adventure of spiritual deepening and self-uncovery. (I learned a long time ago that I was not discovering myself, but uncovering a self that has always been present and available.)

That fateful experience transpired over eighteen years ago. It happened at a point in my life when my fear was at its peak. Bringing a baby into the world and being responsible for her well-being was terrifying to me. I didn't take the vocation of parenting lightly. At the very moment when I most craved order in my life, all hell broke loose. From the chaos came greater chaos.

The chaos did not magically subside with the present-moment miracle I experienced during the crash. However, in retrospect, perhaps the massive chaos was a wake-up call that fueled my desire to create order from the chaos in life—the clutter in my brain. It drove me on a mission to find a way out of the clutter and into greater presence each and every day of my life.

If you have picked up this book, you too are likely suffering from the incessant mental chatter that clutters your brain, sometimes to the point of paralysis. The good news is that it doesn't have to take you the eighteen years that it has taken me to pull the catalogues of past grievances and futuristic doom and gloom fantasies from the overstuffed shelves in your brain. Your journey starts now, with commitment. Are you ready to firmly commit to removing the cluttered cobwebs of self-delusion from the recesses of your mind? If so, then this book is for you. If not, then perhaps it will plant a seed in your psyche that can grow if and when it is time to do so.

Eight Steps to Melt Away the Chaos

In order to support you so that chaos will no longer be the driving factor in your life, I have structured this decluttering program into eight steps. Within each of the steps are profiles and surveys that will assist you in gaining greater clarity about where you stand with particular problem areas (or rather, opportunity areas) in your life. I have also created experiential exercises to help you move through and beyond any blockages that you may find.

Step 1 is *ruthless self-examination*. In order to be fully present, you have to know whom you are being present *with*. In other words, you need to know all of yourself—what you may perceive as the good, the bad, and the ugly.

Step 2 is *commit to inner integrity*. Once you have a greater sense of who you are, you need to dig even deeper, especially to the parts of yourself you struggle with. I have been shocked by the insights I have gained about myself when I asked for support to be more in integrity and to look deeper into my self-manipulations and self-misperceptions.

Step 3 requires you to *step out of victimhood*. This has been one of the most difficult steps for me to take. Life might seem to be much easier when we can attack and blame others for our issues, but this will take us further down the rabbit hole of deeper brain clutter and greater dis-ease in life. Trust me: I learned this the hard way!

Step 4 encourages you to *find the courage to build intimate relationships*. While you may think you already have them, very often what we perceive as intimacy is what I call *intimidacy*. Our relationships can be dysfunctional, based in manipulation and falsehood to support the needs of our egos. Again, this step requires you to do some honest inventory and deeper introspection. Doing so will open a portal to true intimacy in your life—a connection based in healthy independence and honest and heartful interactions.

Step 5 requires you to *ask for help* from others and from the Universe. It takes great courage to look within, and for many of us, it takes even greater courage to make ourselves vulnerable enough to ask others for assistance. This was perhaps the single most difficult step in my journey. It took all of the courage I could muster to say, "I need help." While I told myself that I had no problem asking the Divine for assistance, as I looked deeper, I saw that I could not fully ask if I could not ask my fellow human beings for help as well. In other words, if I didn't believe that I deserved support from my friends and loved ones, how could I believe that I deserved to have the Creator answer my prayers?

In Step 6, constant application of the *Say Yes process* is extremely empowering. It has been monumental in raising my energy and shifting my perceptions. It has helped me manifest the experiences I wanted and has helped me push through negative thinking and into the world of possibilities.

In step 7 I encourage you to *choose an attitude of gratitude*. While I'm sure you have frequently heard about the power of gratitude, I am talking about a gratitude that moves you beyond a simple thank-you. I thought I was an incredibly grateful individual until I looked further and deeper. Then I realized that the gratitude was manipulative. It was a step towards getting something more instead of an authentic expression of thanks for what I was experiencing in the moment.

Step 8 takes you to the place where you can *expect the unexpected*. As you explore this step, you will see more and more miracles abound and synchronicities appear in your life. They are a joy and a tickle! Each time I experience them, I feel as if Santa has taken another journey down the chimney of my heart. The more you are aware of these delights, the more you will experience them. They always exist in the world of potentiality and are waiting for your cues to allow them to manifest in your life.

With each step, I will take you through some of the trappings that your brain uses to ensnarl you into its web of chaos and clutter. The description of each trap will assist you in catching them and witnessing them as they appear in your life. The more you can remain in a witness state with them (as opposed to merely reacting), the less power they will have over you.

As I developed and practiced these eight steps in my life, I gradually saw more and more transformation. I am not promising you a quick fix. Most of us have built a solid foundation of years and years of self-abuse, self-criticism, and self-deception that usually takes time to realize, actualize, and finally work through.

I don't claim to have all of the answers, and my mind is not constantly quiet, but the noise and clutter have subsided considerably. Where I once avoided the quiet at any cost, I now find relief and joy in sitting in silent contemplation and meditation.

In truth, the major shift came after I went to India in 2013 to raise my consciousness and seek further solace. There I was introduced to a spiritual master who single-handedly supported a shift in my consciousness that has been like no other. I will say more about this later.

Don't Just Read, DO!

After over a decade of working as a motivational audio-book producer, my commitment to shifting paradigms and changing lives has become an imperative. Many seekers of higher consciousness find themselves trapped in a cycle of reading the books and attending the webinars and seminars, only to find themselves seeking out their next fix. This can be another brain trap, as our brilliant egos tell us that the next experience outside of our minds will be the one that will heal all wounds and satiate all woes—when this can distract us from doing the emotional and spiritual work that truly raises our consciousness.

For this reason, I start each section with a profile questionnaire and end each with an experiential exercise. When you come to these, I strongly encourage you to stop reading and actually do the profiles and exercises. You may say to yourself, "I'll go back and do them once I've read the book through." More often than not, you will fail to do so. You will grab the next book or attend the next weekend workshop, seeking solace outside of your own internal experience.

Have the courage to stop the cycle now and do each of the exercises as you encounter them. I personally treat books with the greatest respect—so much so that I refuse to use anything but pencil to highlight them (which was a huge challenge at times while I was in university!). I also believe that experiential exercises can be much more powerful if you are able to sit back and be guided through them. For these reasons, I created pdfs of each of the profiles and audio recordings of each of the exercises on my website, so that you can easily download them and use them at your convenience. To access the files, go to www.8WaysToDeclutterYourBrain.com. You will find a tab for Profile Questionnaires, and another tab for Experiential Exercises. Be sure to keep a journal as you go through these processes so that you can record your experiences and track your progress. Doing so will prove to be invaluable!

Decluttering Is Simple, but It's Not Easy!

Before you go any further, I want to remind you that the process of decluttering your brain is simple, but it is not easy. While I provide you with many tools in this book, you have to commit to doing the work. A shift will not happen overnight. You have likely accumulated years of self-destructive beliefs and habits that have infiltrated your brain. It will take time and concentrated effort to declutter it and replace old, ineffective habits with new programming. Be patient with yourself and commit to sticking to it. You are worth it!

As I write this book, I experience moments in which I am suspended in time (as I was during the car awakening). Because these experiences happen organically and take me into the present moment, I have decided to share them with you. Each experience will be in an enclosed box and will be delineated as "A Moment in Time." I hope that you too will start to experience your own wonderful magical moments in time.

Note the Clutter and Commit to Making the Change

Now that I've shared the story of my accident awakening with you, it's time now for you to wake up and to cultivate a life in which you can start to declutter your brain and shift your paradigm.

To start, I suggest you take the following Brain Clutter Inventory Profile. Doing so will help you to establish where you are on your decluttering journey.

Brain Clutter Inventory Profile

This profile has been created to help you gain clarification and knowledge on the state of your brain on a scale of *cluttered* to *clear*. Once you reach the insights shared in this profile, you can begin the decluttering process with greater self-awareness and understanding of the road ahead. For each of the questions that follow, choose the number that most closely aligns with your situation (1 being "not at all" and 10 being "a great deal").

1. How much do you suffer from brain clutter?
1 — 2 — 3 — 4 — 5 — 6 — 7 — 8 — 9 — 10

2. How much do you struggle with sleep loss due to brain clutter that keeps you awake at night or awakens you throughout the night?

1 — 2 — 3 — 4 — 5 — 6 — 7 — 8 — 9 — 10

3. How much do you grapple with focusing throughout your day?

1 — 2 — 3 — 4 — 5 — 6 — 7 — 8 — 9 — 10

4. Do you struggle with meditating or sitting in silence and stillness for at least five minutes?

1 — 2 — 3 — 4 — 5 — 6 — 7 — 8 — 9 — 10

5. In general, is it difficult for you to make decisions?

1 — 2 — 3 — 4 — 5 — 6 — 7 — 8 — 9 — 10

6. How much do you observe your mind repeating worries throughout your day?

1 — 2 — 3 — 4 — 5 — 6 — 7 — 8 — 9 — 10

7. Do you find yourself being more reactive and confrontational than you want to be?

1 — 2 — 3 — 4 — 5 — 6 — 7 — 8 — 9 — 10

8. Are you highly critical of yourself and others?

1 — 2 — 3 — 4 — 5 — 6 — 7 — 8 — 9 — 10

9. Do you struggle with forgiving yourself and others who have wronged you?

1 — 2 — 3 — 4 — 5 — 6 — 7 — 8 — 9 — 10

10. Do you seek change but struggle to act on new information?

1 — 2 — 3 — 4 — 5 — 6 — 7 — 8 — 9 — 10

If you scored between 76 and 100, there is a great deal of room to shift your life in a less cluttered and more positive direction. Choosing to go through this book at this time in your life's journey can help you move forward with greater insights, tools, and experiential exercises. Give yourself a pat on the back for taking initiative, and know that you are taking steps towards less brain clutter and greater self-love and acceptance.

If you scored between 51 and 75, you have taken some initiative to make shifts in your life, and you are on the road to experiencing greater self-awareness and declutter. Continue by taking routine, daily baby steps, being sure not to overbook your schedule. The more small steps you take, the greater the results you will achieve and the more inspired you will become.

If you scored between 26 and 50, you are on your way to simplifying your life; your brain is only partially cluttered. You are far from being a novice at integrating emotional empowerment practices into your daily routine. Continue to search, and be sure to take steps that will move you beyond understanding and into absolute knowing. In doing so, you will create space for improvements in your life.

If you scored between 10 and 25, congratulations! You have already made great progress in decluttering your brain. You are well on your way to paving a life of

greater ease, peace, creativity, receptivity, and innovation. Using the tools in this book can support you
on the extraordinary path you have already carved for
yourself. Keep up the good work!

Lean In and Look Deeper!

Did you learn anything new about yourself from doing
your Brain Clutter Inventory? Now that you have
opened this energetic portal, you will likely start to
experience more and more ways in which your brain
is cluttered and chaos presides in your life.

Don't panic. Your heightened awareness of the
chaos is the storm before the calm. Note that there is
not more chaos in your life, but that you are choosing
to look squarely at it in order to develop a healthier
relationship with it.

As I previously outlined, there are eight ways in
which you can start the decluttering process. You may
already be implementing some of them. If so, great!
However, I encourage you to look deeper, even into
areas in which you feel you have already completed
your emotional work.

Our personality-self (also called the *ego* or the
lower self) is very crafty. It is the part of us that is fear-
based. We tend to be reactive and in a constant state
of fight-or-flight. Although we may be unaware of it,
the ego drains us and keeps us stuck on what we fear
the most. If it gets out of control, it can paralyze us and
literally manifest that which we fear the most.

After years of peeling away the layers of my ego's tricks and traps, for the most part I thought I had it calmed. However, the more I asked Universal Source for insights, the more I saw that I still had even more to experience and understand (even in the areas where I was sure I had overcome my issues and quelled any concerns).

A Moment in Time

I just had an experience that shocked me into a state of heightened awareness. To provide you with an example of taking the work that I do into my experience, here is what happened and how I processed the experience.

I was preparing a cup of tea in the teachers' break room. I had a run of my solo theatrical production coming up. Taking all of the courage I could muster at the time, I held some information postcards up and said to a group of about eight teachers, "If any of you are at all interested in theater, I have a five-week run of my solo show coming up." While they looked at me, not one of them responded. Not a word! Not even a smile or a nod of recognition. I was both shocked and embarrassed. Here's how I processed the experience:

1. I witnessed them in the exchange, and then I bore witness to myself. I walked over to my bubbling kettle until it boiled, unable to take my eyes off it. While I felt into my feelings at that moment,

I also watched myself as if I were observing a film. I continued to witness and feel until I was out of the room.

2. When I was alone, I allowed myself to feel into the feelings in a deeper way. I began to cry. I realized that I was awkward about self-promotion in the first place, and my ego had told me that this was further proof that I was unworthy and an imposition.

3. As I cried, I did not judge the thoughts or the feelings that arose within me. I allowed them to have full expression.

4. Once the tears stopped, I later noted the anger I felt as one of the teachers later passed me in the hall and said, "Hello." I barely responded. I judged her coldness. I watched.

5. Later a memory came up for me. Years ago, I was attending a football game at my alma mater. As I sat in the bleachers, a young man appeared among the flag dancers. He was dancing his heart out. Because young men were typically not dancers, I noted a couple of people around me snickering. Then I noted the mob laughing. Finally, as I watched, I could see and feel the sadness and embarrassment that arose within him. He felt like an outcast. I then linked that experience to the one I had today. I too felt like an outcast—ashamed and alone. I simply noted and observed.

6. I later noted the sense of psychospiritual superiority that arose within me after seeing the teacher in the hall. I thought, "She is not very evolved, not at all conscious. None of them were, to be so rude and unresponsive." I just witnessed and noted my hurt turning to judgment, with compassion for myself. (In all honesty, I was not in a place where I could authentically feel compassion towards the teachers. I may in time, but I had to be with what was without trying to manipulate myself out of my anger and sadness.)

Now that I have committed to this experience as a means of learning more about myself and healing some of the woundedness that I feel, I know that residual thoughts and feelings will arise in response. I will continue to observe, being sure to have compassion for myself throughout.

One gift I received was appreciation for you, the reader. Many if not most of the people living on this planet do so blindly. For whatever reason, they have not made any effort to raise their consciousness. They are lost in their own maze of brain clutter and have made no attempt to find a way out. This is not judgment, but observation. I know many who are so deeply hurting that they cannot see the part that they themselves play in their life's dramas. Their pain is deep, and their denial is deeper. They have thick armor protecting their sad hearts.

You, as a committed truth seeker, are not in the majority, but the impact you have is vast. Never underestimate the power that you hold. I see your commitment, and I acknowledge you for having the courage, discipline, and perseverance to see it through. You want to fall in love with yourself, and your commitment is commendable. On behalf of all of those whom you have unknowingly touched in your life, in your commitment to being the most expansive person you can be, I say a heartfelt, "Thank you! Thank you! Thank you!" You have no idea the impact that you are making on this earth now and for generations to come.

Introduction

Preparing for Your Journey of Decluttering

Before we delve into your journey, I would like to suggest several things that may help you deconstruct your current patterns and clean out the cobwebs of clutter from your brain.

The first premise I would like to share is this: *your beliefs become your reality.* You may already be familiar with this precept from the well-known concept of the Law of Attraction. In any event, we will explore this powerful law throughout this book.

How do I know that our beliefs become our reality? All I can point to—emphatically and without hesitation—is my own experience. Throughout my life, I have noted that the deeper I felt this belief, the more my life experience would model it—so much so that I have no doubt that my beliefs do in fact create my reality.

I also believe, with all my heart and soul, that this universe is benevolent and supports us. Our failure to realize this truth and our own sense of unworthiness are the only things that stop us from experiencing deep inner peace and a life that is filled with the wonders created by alignment with Source. I feel extremely blessed, as incredible things have manifested in my life. I'll be sharing some stories about them, but I want you to be able to manifest the same things yourself. I look forward to supporting you to the point where you know without a doubt that you too are not alone and that you have the knowledge and resources to manifest what you've only dreamt of in your life.

One Energy, Many Names

When I first arrived in Chicago, I had the good fortune to work at Nightingale-Conant Corporation, which at the time was the world's largest motivational audiobook publisher. I was blessed in being able to work with some of the most extraordinary spiritual masters of the twenty-first century, and I was exposed to a plethora of spiritual traditions and belief systems.

Ultimately I learned that there is one core Truth, which is the root of just about all of those spiritual practices. There is a Presence that supports our existence in a profound and potent way. It is highly creative, benevolent, and mysterious. Each tradition celebrates it in a different way.

I laugh at myself sometimes, remembering that throughout my childhood and much of my adult life, I believed that divinity was a punitive old man who sat on a cloud and tracked my progress on my life's report card, punishing me when I made mistakes and rewarding me when I did good. After years of humanizing and compartmentalizing that creative force, I realized that my limited human mind had difficulty comprehending anything beyond human frailties and conditional love. So, to relate this Presence to my world, I made it human—critic and all.

I now believe that my one and only critic is *me*. There is no disappointed old man—just a huge, loving force that cocreates my world alongside me. As I learn to release my inner critic and sit as the witness to the happenings in my life, this truth becomes clearer and clearer.

It doesn't matter whether you believe that you are that divine force yourself or you believe it exists outside of you. It doesn't matter how you celebrate or honor your existence. Whatever religious tradition you follow (or don't follow) has no bearing on your ability to declutter your mind and manifest the life you want to cocreate for yourself (note that I said *co*create!).

Throughout this book, you will see me referencing that creative force as the *Universe*. You could see yourself as divine, or you could also experience it as "my Divine," "God," "Goddess," "Universal Source," "Gaia," "Source," "Pachamama," "my Soul," "Yahweh," "Supreme Intelligence," "Jesus," "The Christ," "Holy Spirit," "Truth," "Allah," "Buddha," or a million other names. What you or I call it does not matter. What matters is that when I refer to it in this book, it resonates with you.

Some of my spiritual mentors have suggested that, if we see the Creative Force as something or someone outside of ourselves, we first need to build a personal and intimate relationship with them or it. Once our consciousness is raised, we will start to experience that energy as a Force that is rooted within each of us. To be honest with you, I'm not there yet, but I am well on my way. While in my head, I believe that Divinity is within me, the rest of me has not caught up yet. I celebrate that Creative Force as several masters from whom I seek guidance: Jesus; Mother Mary; Buddha; the Buddhist deity Quan Yin; Pachamama, the earth mother goddess of the Andean peoples; and the Indian spiritual master Sri Amma Bhagavan. For I believe they all knew that they were that Creativity, and that, in time, I will as well.

As you start this journey with me, what is most important is that your heart and mind are open. Translate my spiritual or creative connections into whatever applies to your belief system. Take what resonates with you, ponder what does not, and let go of that which does not serve you.

Thoughts Are Not Mine; They Just Are!

One of the most powerful experiences I've ever had was attending the Oneness University near Chennai, India, for a month-long workshop with Sri Amma

Bhagavan. One of the most profound and mind-altering lessons from this master, who I believe is enlightened, was that we are not our minds. That which we think is a part of the *thoughtmosphere*, as much as the air we breathe is part of the atmosphere.

Several years prior to going to India, I was graced to produce several audiobooks with the late Dr. David Hawkins, author of numerous books including *Power versus Force*. Beyond a shadow of a doubt, I know that he was an enlightened soul.

When I first interviewed him during our preliminary recording session, I was confused by his verbiage. Whenever he spoke, he would say "*the* mind," as opposed to "*my* mind," and to "*the* body," as opposed to "*my* body." He always referred to them in the third person. Now, years later, I understand why he did. He knew that he was not his mind or his body. Moreover, he experienced what he was *not*. While I may know that I am not this mind or body, I still have not fully experienced it.

He knew and was modeling the fact that a vast part of conscious growth is moving beyond personal identification. Much of this process happens naturally when you cultivate the witness-self. That is why meditation is so powerful. Watching the thoughts as they flow in and out of your brain, you start to experience them like a movie that is playing. You start to realize that you are the watcher of the thoughts, not the thinker. They come and go. You do not plan or create them. As you continue to focus on witnessing, you start to see the trappings that the mind has created in order to have you buy into the premise that you are the thoughts that run through your brain.

If in fact the thoughts we think are not ours, then we are *not* those thoughts. When I heard this, I was flabbergasted. I realized that I believed with all of my heart that I was the thoughts that I think. In response, I labeled myself. I reflected on the guilt and self-criticism I felt after years of believing that my thoughts made me the person I am today.

If you are not your thoughts, then who are you? If you realize that you are not responsible for the thoughts, then how does this new paradigm shift your beliefs about yourself and others?

When You Heal Yourself, You Heal the World
Now that I've planted the seed (the idea that you are not your thoughts), let's start to dismantle what the clutter in your brain has been telling you. Once you see how your thoughts have been holding you prisoner in a whirlwind of self-criticism and spiraling ego games, you can move past them into a life of greater peace and joy.

Set an intention to become a model for friends, family, and others in the world, who will note the shifts you have made and will ask, "What the heck is going on with you?" Note that when you change, you affect change the world over. As Malcolm Gladwell reminds us in his mind-altering book *The Tipping Point: How Little Things Make a Big Difference*, "Look at the world around you. It may seem like an immovable, implacable place. It is not. With the slightest push—in just the right place—it can be tipped."

Grappling with Your Desires for Material Gain

Bhagavan shared the invaluable insight that we need to stop shaming ourselves for our material wants. He said that his most successful students seeking to gain higher consciousness and eventual enlightenment have been successful businessmen and women, because they have already satiated their worldly desires. They have attained power, wealth, and fame and fulfilled all of their earthly yearnings. After doing so, they were ready to ask the question, *"Now* what?" They were led on a speedy path to higher consciousness because they had already fulfilled the list of what their brains told them they wanted in order to experience peace and joy. If they had not been on that previous quest to alleviate their ego's drives, they might not have reached the point of wanting to look deeper within to find true peace.

If you have worldly wants, you can try to force yourself to detach from wanting, or you can follow your desires to greater wisdom and self-awareness. The choice is yours. However, you may find that the "shoulding all over yourself" never ends. So why not allow your desires to lead you without shame and guilt and see how the Universe supports your outer and inner journey?

Manifesting Works Both Ways!

One of my greatest blessings is the ease with which manifestations occur in my life. I never realized this until I was attending a retreat that was being held by two of the coaches I hired at Nightingale-Conant. They motioned toward me and said to the audience, "If you ever want to meet someone who has been blessed and manifests, talk to Theresa."

I then realized just how blessed I have been throughout my life. Manifestations have come my way in abundance. That being said, I also learned that being a manifester (which we all have the capacity to be) has great power, with both beneficial and challenging aspects. You have the ability to manifest that which you *don't* want with just as much ease as that which you *do* want. Thus you need to take care of the thoughts you think and the words you use. Choose wisely!

The Dance of Dichotomies

I will spend a good part of this book dissecting the dichotomies with which the ego clutters our brains. If you're a spiritual seeker, as I am, your mind can play really powerful tricks. In fact, sometimes I wonder, "Is there a correlation between the depth of our spiritual commitment and the ingenuity of our minds? Is it true that the more committed we are, the more brilliant and crazy-making our mind traps are?"

A couple of examples of this mind game: I noted that I was feeling guilty about the feelings of guilt I had all the time. I felt that with all of the work I did, I should be over the guilt cycle. I also noted that I was being unforgiving with myself about being so unforgiving. I have learned that unforgiveness burns my energy and only hurts me. While I know this truth in my mind, it has been difficult to integrate into my life. The self-critical message that reels around in my brain is *you know better*! The more I worked on shifting things, the crazier the messages became. Under the guise of emotional improvement, I was trapping myself into even deeper self-incrimination.

Sometimes the Ego Needs a Good, Solid Bruise

A few years ago, I realized that I was in a job that was no longer fulfilling. Although I was paid very well and I was using many of my skills, I realized that I had outgrown it and that it was no longer a fit.

I started setting my intentions with great clarity and commitment. I knew it was time to leave, but I didn't want to quit. At that time, my belief was that I couldn't afford it financially. So I did what I often do and had a conversation in my head: "OK, Universe, let me out of here, but in a way that will be supportive, both physically and emotionally." I was feeling trapped. While wanting to leave, I didn't want to be fired or laid off.

I got my wish—to a degree. Within a couple of months, the company had a huge layoff. I was thrilled and devastated at the same time. My ego screamed, "Wait a second. I'm superwoman. I'm too good to be laid off. This can't be happening to me." Every night for several months I had nightmares about the layoff, but ultimately I had gotten what I wanted. Because it was a large staff layoff, I was given a severance and unemployment benefits. The conditions for leaving could not have been better. Although the ego struggled, as I look back at the situation, I realize that getting laid off was the best thing that could have happened to me.

While my fragile sense of self had been rocked, one of my wise spiritual teachers said, "Theresa, you'll get over it. Your spirit, your soul is bigger than the ego. The ego is bruised, but the soul knows." I have no doubt that my soul (or the benevolent Universal Cocreator) orchestrated the whole thing. I believe without a doubt that the Universe was saying, "OK, girl. Put your money where your mouth is. We're going to take you on this journey, and you're going to get this done."

From Productive Procrastination to Creation

Several years prior to leaving the job, I had drafted seven children's books. They had been sitting, collecting dust in my brain and on my aging computer. I finally committed to getting them printed and produced.

I have to confess that for the first several months, I busied myself in what I call "productive procrastination." I am an expert at it. When I have a pending deadline, I accomplish everything that has been waiting for years. I cleaned out closets, organized shoes, finished the myriad of painting and repair jobs around the house and completed just about every project I could come up with before sinking my teeth into the real creations that I wanted to manifest. Sound familiar? Again, this is another trick of the brain that keeps us busy and prevents us from just doing it!

I made a point of leaving the house for the day, sometimes heading to a nearby coffee shop or library. At home there were too many opportunities to get lost in productive procrastination. I also committed myself to staying away from the television. While I had one, I did not set it up for viewing, other than the odd film that I would rent. I realized that I could easily spend hours each day sitting listlessly in front of the screen, getting none of my work done.

Once I finally sank my teeth into getting the books done and out, in no time at all I found a terrific illustrator, and a printing company for my Terri series of books.

Since the layoff, I have made another couple of career moves, but I have never looked back. I've been living the dreams that I've wanted to live. It's time I shared this gift with you, because you can experience it too.

The Twin Serpents Speak

This book began several years ago as an audio program that I recorded with my dear friend, Theresa Cordova. While I wanted to create it, I kept thinking, "I'm not ready. I don't have it all written out, and it's not perfect yet, so I can't do it." So I had a conversation with the Universe: "OK, Universe, it's time for me to do this book. I don't think I'm ready yet, but I need a sign. Maybe I should wait another year, maybe two years." A little voice was inside me saying, *"No. Now, now, now,"* but I still hesitated, waiting for that sign.

A couple of days later, my dear friend and spiritual mentor Jackie Mellen guided me through a meditation. After completing it, she said, "Theresa, your spirit guides were singing a song: 'It's Now or Never.' Does that mean anything to you?" I started laughing, and I said, "I don't know the rest of the song, but I don't think I need to!"

That night I had a dream. In the dream, I was walking along a street in Arizona, and there were two yellow and white serpents, which approached me and bit into each of my arms. I previously learned that the serpent represents an initiation into a deeper spiritual journey. When they come into our dreams (and they often appear in mine), our job is not to fear them, but to encourage them to bite us. So I did not resist.

A Moment in Time

As I sit here in a café in suburban Chicago, I stop and watch. A mother is walking with her beautiful little daughter. She is about three years old and is in awe of everything. I watch in wonder, gratitude, and joy. For a moment I find myself walking in the child's shoes, delighted that I get to push the button that will magically change the red traffic light to green. No fears about tomorrow, nor any regrets about yesterday. She is present, and for a moment, I am with her, present and awe-inspired. My heart is filled with joy and appreciation.

For a moment, I did not worry about the outcome of this book. I did not fret about the words I am typing or the time lost in productive procrastination. I was present, and perhaps that was the purpose for this day.

Within a year, I was at a studio in Cottonwood, Arizona, recording the audio that was the first version of this book. My intentions were heard, and the signs were manifest.

Had I not been laid off, I would not have had the time or the financial wherewithal to complete either project. The Universe had my back, and my ego survived the wounds.

I also realized that I am one of millions of talented individuals in the world. While we are each unique and bring our own sense of self to the job, none of us is irreplaceable in the business world.

What Messages Do You Need to Hear?

Dialogue with the Universe is now a constant in my life. I am often guided to take steps that make no logical sense to me. I find that without fail, I always regret the times that I don't heed the messages and follow the signs. In order to do this divine dance, you have to believe that the Universe is messaging you, and you have to listen for these messages. Then you need to act on them. If you don't, your trust in yourself and the universal support that responds to you will dull and eventually dissipate.

You've probably had insights or premonitions, but you didn't follow through on them. Later you've said, "I knew that I should have done it." So I'm going to encourage you: start doing it now!

Busyness and Brain Clutter—Your Ego's Greatest Allies

It can be difficult to begin to take action, if we don't take the time to slow down and ask. One behavior that we frequently overutilize is staying too busy. The world is speeding up, and things are getting faster and faster.

I started a job in downtown Chicago. In the suburbs, I was the speed walker. Nobody could walk as fast as me. I'd keep up with the runners, but I couldn't keep up with some of Chicago's commuters. They sure could move!

The world is so fast that you need to consciously and deliberately slow down and listen. (Actually, it never ceases to amaze me how those incredible messages were able to penetrate my consciousness despite my busyness and my cluttered, noisy mind, and despite the fact that I didn't meditate very much in those years.) The key is listening even when you have many distractions and commitments in your life.

To Buy or Not to Buy: That Is the Question

How do you know if the messages you're hearing are from the Universe or from your ego? Recently I had to decide whether I was going to buy a house. My ego was saying, "Wait a second. There are deals right now; mortgages are low; you have this money, you need to buy." Should, should, should.

A wonderful channeler that I know told me, "Stop. Take a moment and experience this from your ten-year-old vantage point." She had me breathe into buying a home. She said, "When you breathe into buying this home, do you see a fireplace? Does that warm your heart? Do you see the kind of kitchen and backyard that you want? Is there a sense of security and joy? Does it give you giggles and tickles?"

I experienced the house in my mind's eye, and I realized, "No. Right now I want the money I have from the house I just sold to support my books and my one-woman show. I don't want a house right now. I don't get excited by a fireplace and a backyard." There was my answer.

Exercise 1: Stop, Breathe, and Listen

What are you indecisive about at this moment? What has you burning a great deal of your energy as you pace back and forth in a web of indecision?

Stop and take a deep breath in and out. Take another breath in, and release anything that's going on in that monkey mind of yours. Just let it go. Tighten every muscle in your body, from head to toe. Tighten, tighten, tighten, and relax. Do this three times. Feel into your body. Feel the tension melt with every out-breath. Allow yourself to become present.

Breathe deeply, letting out all of your anxieties, all of your thoughts on the exhale. Now breathe in love. See that love as radiant white light at the center of your heart. See it growing on every inhale. Breathe out all anxieties and tensions on each exhale. See that light growing throughout your body, permeating every organ, every cell of your being.

Now think of something you're undecided about in your life, something that's been burning in your heart and your mind, and about which you've been weighing the odds back and forth.

Imagine yourself as a ten-year-old child, full of joy, uncontained, full of the wonder of the world. Breathe that ten-year-old child into yourself. See yourself as that child, moving ahead on this issue. Give your child time to fully experience it. Then ask that child, "If you do this, and make this choice, how do you feel?"

Watch her energy. Is she excited? Is she joyful? Is she full of anticipation? Or not? If there's another side to the coin, ask that child, "How does *this* feel?" Really feel into it with all of your being. Does this alternative bring joy and excitement? Does it bring a sense of heaviness or trepidation?

Listen to that ten-year-old child and note her response. Thank your ten-year-old self for her guidance. When you feel ready, open your eyes.

This is a very simple exercise. If you're weighted down with "should I or shouldn't I?" you can stop. You can take thirty to forty seconds, go to your younger self and ask, "How does this make me feel?" If it brings joy, then do it. If it doesn't, then you have your answer: not right now.

Step 1

Ruthless Self-Examination

To empower yourself, you need to believe.

The first thing to do is to say, "OK, Universe, here's the deal. I want to be conscious of these obstacles. I want to start fixing them, but I can't fix them if I don't see them. Please show them to me."

If you absolutely believe that the Universe will start bringing these up for you, it will. If you don't believe it, you might as well put this book down right now.

You have to believe, and that belief sets transformation in motion. The Universal Creative Force will show up to support you. You'll start receiving messages and information; you'll start having dreams. These blockages will start to show themselves. When they do, you can take the steps necessary to heal them.

You Must Be Clear about Your Needs

Once you ask for your consciousness to be raised, you will be shown everything to the degree of your asking—what you want to see and what you don't want to see.

Before delving further into "seeing," it is important to take some time to assess your needs. Without being crystal-clear on exactly what your needs are, you cannot begin to do the decluttering process.

Wants Assessment Profile

To unencumber yourself from any blocks that might be keeping you from manifesting what you desire, it helps to become clear about what they are and what need you believe they fulfill.

Separating wants from needs helps free you from some of the burdensome pressures you put on yourself. Once I realized that I did not have many needs, the weight of brain clutter lightened, and I felt less stressed.

This profile will help you clarify your needs in comparison to your wants. For each of the questions, choose the number that is most closely aligns to your situation (1 being "not at all" and 10 being "a great deal").

1. Are you currently struggling to meet your basic needs in your life?

1 — 2 — 3 — 4 — 5 — 6 — 7 — 8 — 9 — 10

2. Do you judge yourself for desiring too much in your life?

1 — 2 — 3 — 4 — 5 — 6 — 7 — 8 — 9 — 10

3. Do you judge others who experience abundance in their lives?

1 — 2 — 3 — 4 — 5 — 6 — 7 — 8 — 9 — 10

4. Do you often find yourself jealous of those who struggle less than you?

1 — 2 — 3 — 4 — 5 — 6 — 7 — 8 — 9 — 10

5. Have you ever wished you were living another person's life?

1 — 2 — 3 — 4 — 5 — 6 — 7 — 8 — 9 — 10

6. Do you spend much time stewing about what you don't have in your life, and less time having fun?

1 — 2 — 3 — 4 — 5 — 6 — 7 — 8 — 9 — 10

7. Eating out with friends, do you find yourself tallying up bills to the penny, then feeling resentful if others fall short?

1 — 2 — 3 — 4 — 5 — 6 — 7 — 8 — 9 — 10

8. Do you struggle to enlist the support of others with your business ventures?

1 — 2 — 3 — 4 — 5 — 6 — 7 — 8 — 9 — 10

9. Do you worry about not fulfilling your soul's calling in your life?

1 — 2 — 3 — 4 — 5 — 6 — 7 — 8 — 9 — 10

10. Do you spend more time worrying, and less time visualizing your success?

1 — 2 — 3 — 4 — 5 — 6 — 7 — 8 — 9 — 10

If you scored between 76 and 100, you are experiencing a great deal of emotional pain around your feelings of lack. Know that you are not alone and that there is a way to take yourself out of discouragement and into hope.

Start by spending one minute each morning as you arise, focusing on the things you are most grateful for in your life. Know that the gratitude will grow and will help to pull you from helplessness to hope.

If you scored between 51 and 75, you have started taking steps towards discerning what your needs are compared to your wants. Allow yourself to feel your feelings around lack, jealousy, and judgment, having compassion for yourself. Then take yourself to the place of imagining how a life of abundance (financial, relational, etc.) would feel, being sure to use your senses and experience the delight, as if it were happening here and now.

If you scored between 26 and 50, you are well on your way to manifesting the life that you were meant to live. Continue to be honest with yourself about your sense of lack. When you catch yourself experience jealousy or a sense of "not enough," have compassion for yourself, as you would a young child. Trust that you are well on your way to greater manifestation, and bathe in the strides you have already made towards removing blocks in your life.

If you scored between 10 and 25, congratulations! You have a great deal of clarity about what your wants are, and you are well on your way to manifesting them in your life. You have clearly been working on manifesting and you have removed a great many of the blocks to experiencing the life you desire. Continue to look at what you have in your life, expressing gratitude for what is, as you allow yourself to feel into even more manifesting in your life.

It's OK to Want It All

Now that you have completed your wants assessment, take an inventory of your discoveries. Do you have more wants than you are comfortable with? Less? Are your wants what you anticipated they would be? Any surprises?

One game my brain plays on me is to shame me about my volume of wants. There is a critical voice in my head that yells, "You say you are on a spiritual path, yet look at your long list of wants. You are such a hypocrite. If you truly were spiritual, you would want nothing." Ouch! Sound familiar?

A strong idea that permeates the thoughtmosphere is "You want it all. Well, you can't have it all!" I've heard it from parents and peers, but most frequently within my own mind. As you watch a child light up in anticipation of a massive ice-cream cone, do you judge that child? If that child wants huge loads of colorful sprinkles on her ice cream, do you judge her? Do you quell her enthusiasm? I don't think so.

Wants versus Needs

To create further clarity, we can separate our wants from our needs. Frank Mallinder, a wonderful personal coach I had for several years, posed a provocative question during one of our sessions: "If your house was burning down, what would you absolutely have to take with you?"

Take a moment to ask yourself the same question. You may be surprised. After considering it, I was! I realized that the only items that would be of value to me were two scrapbooks that I had created for my daughter. I created one soon after she was born, and another during her second and third years. Each book contained poems that I wrote, along with artwork. I creatively poured every ounce of my love for her into those books. My parents came down to Chicago to stay with me during her first month. I played and prayed over those books during the months of postpartum depression, through the challenging and lonely times in Chicago without my family, throughout the frightening days of 9/11 (she was less than a month old when the towers fell), to the days when I finally got too busy between work and childcare to continue adding to them.

They were the only items I absolutely wanted to take with me. I was shocked at the realization that they were all I truly cherished. However, that doesn't prevent me from dreaming of having a beautiful house with a magically landscaped garden and tranquility pool someday. We each have our needs and wants. We may be able to survive on very little, but we should make every effort not to judge ourselves for wanting.

Sing Your Song Despite That Inner Critic

Several years ago, I had an experience with my daughter. Singing was her absolute dream. So I found her a singing teacher that I thought was skilled and professional. However, within twenty minutes of starting her first session, the instructor discouraged my daughter.

My daughter was devastated. Having been in similar situations in my life, I pondered her predicament, and in the end I told her that she had one of three choices.

Choice 1: She could choose defeat, make the teacher right, and never sing again. If she chose this path, however, she would undoubtedly experience regret about the passion that was not pursued, and anger at the teacher to whom she forfeited her passion and power.

Choice 2: She could become vengeful and say to herself, "I'm going to show her." In this case, she could spend the rest of her life anxious and angry, working her tail off to prove the teacher wrong. This choice is often energetically draining, and because it is stoked in negativity, no matter the outcome, it most often leads to bitterness and resentment.

Choice 3: She could follow through on her plan and do what she loves *despite* what the misguided teacher said. In this case, her love and passion are in the driver's seat. This choice takes courage and strength. She has to follow her heart and disempower the naysayers. I've made this choice a lot in my life, and while it hasn't been easy, I've never regretted making it!

Failing at Failure

For most, *failure* is a dirty word. However, when you study the innovators and shakers in history, you discover that most of them failed many times. In fact, they welcomed failure as an opportunity to continue their work towards success.

Being a perfectionist, I realized that if I was going to grow emotionally, I would need to be OK with failure in my life.

In the early 2000s, I wrote a study guide for an audiobook, *The 28 Principles of Attraction*, for the late personal-coaching guru Thomas Leonard. He was an amazing man, and he did remarkable work to create the personal and professional coaching empire.

One exercise he suggested was to allow ourselves to fail. If we were uncomfortable with failure, we should intentionally make mistakes as an exercise in emotional growth.

It was a potent exercise. I remember intentionally making errors when writing, or intentionally dropping a piece of litter on the sidewalk. It was difficult for me to do. I soon noted the clutter that had taken over my brain around the exercise: "You're failing at failure. It's not working, and you are not working!" I realized how difficult it was for me to color outside the lines in the doodling book of my existence. It was further evidence of the nasty games that the ego mind was playing on me.

A Moment in Time

"The summer wind came blowin' in . . . "

I'm always amazed at the creativity of the Universe and how it responds to my summons. Upon completion of the last paragraph, I headed to the local library to continue writing. As I entered, my ears melted, along with my heart. A young man stood over an eighty-four-year old gentleman. The young man held his cell phone against the other man's ear. As Frank Sinatra crooned in the background, the elderly man sang his full, open-throated version of "Summer Wind." He had a wonderful voice, and I could feel his unencumbered joy. He was proud of his voice and clearly loved music. He did not care who listened; he had no fears of being scrutinized or judged. He was at one with the music and was living joy. Another delectable moment to experience as summer's wind welcomes the falling leaves of autumn.

After a time, I stopped intentionally failing. Now I note the failures when they occur, and I try to move on without bullying myself. It helps to tell myself, "I did not know better. If I knew better, I would have made better choices." This has given me greater compassion towards others. I realized that I have no idea where they have been, or where they are going. Until I walk a lifetime in their shoes, I cannot know why they do what they do. Similarly, if they have not walked in mine, it is difficult for them to judge fairly.

Failing to See Divorce as a Failure

Several years ago, I knew my marriage was over, but I had the view of divorce as a huge failure, to the point where I saw divorced individuals as wounded, messed up souls. My marriage counselor pointed my prejudice out to me, and I explored it for a while.

After many years and way too many marriage counselors, I got to the point where I really hated the person I had become in the marriage. I was angry and bitter. No matter what I did, I was unable to shake my bitterness and knew that ending the marriage was the best I could do at the time.

As I was going through the ugly, vicious, tit-for-tat arguments and legal battles that many divorcees endure, I started journaling. I was performing in a show at that time, and each evening, before rehearsals or performances, I would sit in the green room and write, and write, and write.

I would imagine the life I wanted, and I would feel into it, describing it in great detail. I would see a harmonious breakup. I would envision my wasband and me as friendly, unconflicted coparents. I would envision a postdivorce relationship that many would consider impossible. After about six months of doing this, I thought, "This is not working. The divorce is not happening the way I've been visualizing. In fact, it's been a disaster!" I got angry at the Universe and said, "Wait a second, Universe. I've been doing my homework, but you're not following the lead. What's going on here?"

All in divine time, because two years later, I realized that every single thing that I had written down had manifested. As is often the case, my requests were not answered at the time I anticipated, nor did they come in the package I expected. But when I look back, I saw that the lessons I learned along the way were really valuable. In retrospect, they were always perfect. The challenge was to let go of my agenda and allow it all to transpire as it should. It's a matter of trust and divine timing. The Universe responded in its own perfect way, despite my efforts to control and have things my way. Had I let go of my agenda, however, the road would have been much smoother.

I encourage you to do the following exercise when you want to manifest something in your life but are too paralyzed to act. You might also want to work with something you feel you *have* already failed at. Go through this exercise and see yourself succeed at your endeavor, and by doing so, you may rewrite that program in your subconscious.

I also encourage you to start writing out what you really want, but the key is to totally *feel into* it as you do so. If you can't experience it in your mind's eye, you may have additional blocks that need attention. I will provide you with some other exercises further on to help you do so.

Exercise 2: If Failure Is Not an Option

Take several deep breaths. Tighten all of the muscles in your body three times and then relax them. Relax your entire body. As you inhale, see white light flooding into your heart and radiating out into every cell of your being. Now watch the voices, the messages coming up in your mind. Just allow them to be present, to come and go. Ask yourself, "What would I do if I could do anything in the world and know that I would never fail at it? What would I do?"

Failure is not an option. See yourself doing it. Feel yourself doing it. You're doing it. There's great joy. There's laughter. You're wonderfully connected with other people. You feel incredible love for yourself. You are honoring and proud of who you are and of what you're doing. You are a model for others as they watch you fulfilling this dream.

They watch you, and their lives change as well. One life after another begins to change, and you are living it. Note how your body feels. How does success taste? How does it smell? Feel into your body right now. Where are you feeling this joy percolating in your body? Where is it flowing?

See yourself achieving the greatest success, whatever that might be, whether you win an award, whether it's financial freedom, free time to do what you really want to do, or connection with other people. You have a sense of your divinity, your highest self. You are living that now, and so it is.

The trick is totally feeling into your vision. Years ago, affirmations were very popular in the personal empowerment arena. You would sit in front of the mirror repeating, "I love myself, I love myself, I love myself." Then you wondered why it didn't work. Merely speaking it is not enough. You have to feel into it with all of the senses.

Fearing the Fear

Fearing the fear that you experience is a great way to trap yourself into an infinite cycle of brain clutter. In this chapter, I'm going to discuss how to deal with that fear as it may pop up, so that it doesn't dominate your life.

What do I mean by "fearing the fear"? The spiritual text known as *A Course in Miracles* teaches us that there are only two emotions: fear and love. You're either experiencing one or the other, and your actions are based on one or the other. I always touted myself as a very courageous woman, but the more I witnessed and reflected, the more I saw how much fear was ruling my life. I realized that I was literally getting fearful about the fact that I was fearful. How is this possible?

If you have been seeking higher consciousness, you have likely been introduced to the Law of Attraction. This law stipulates that you will attract what you focus on; thus it encourages us to focus on what we want. After studying this theory for some time, I found myself getting fearful, then I would note the fear and panic, because my focus was on fear: "Oh, no. I'm going to manifest lack because I'm focusing on what I don't have—what's *not* in my bank account. I have to shift and focus on what I want. I see abundance . . . Dang, I'm still looking at my bank account and feeling fear. Oh, no. I can't experience fear, or that will create more for me to be afraid of in my life!" You see how the ego creates a vicious cycle of fear clutter in your brain?

Fear Inventory Profile

Most of us suffer more from fear than we realize. In fact, I believe that fear is at the root of most of our problems and is one of the greatest hurdles for mankind to overcome. This profile has been created to help you gain greater clarity on how much fear rules your life.

Like me, you may find that as you peel away your fears, you discover more and more of them. These discoveries are good news. Without awareness of them, you cannot overcome them. With each question, you would best serve yourself by taking a breath and rooting yourself in inner integrity before responding. For each of the questions below, choose the number that most closely aligns to your situation (1 being "not at all" and 10 being "a great deal").

1. Fear runs at the core of most of the decisions I make in my life.

1 — 2 — 3 — 4 — 5 — 6 — 7 — 8 — 9 — 10

2. I rarely take initiative if I am at all fearful about a decision.

1 — 2 — 3 — 4 — 5 — 6 — 7 — 8 — 9 — 10

3. I usually investigate ad nauseam and then choose not to act on something that creates fear within me.

1 — 2 — 3 — 4 — 5 — 6 — 7 — 8 — 9 — 10

4. I avoid change in my life.

1 — 2 — 3 — 4 — 5 — 6 — 7 — 8 — 9 — 10

5. I avoid extending myself beyond my comfort zone.

1 — 2 — 3 — 4 — 5 — 6 — 7 — 8 — 9 — 10

6. Most of my friends tend to be stationary and risk-averse.

1 — 2 — 3 — 4 — 5 — 6 — 7 — 8 — 9 — 10

7. When traveling, I stay on course and do little exploring.

1 — 2 — 3 — 4 — 5 — 6 — 7 — 8 — 9 — 10

8. I get angry if I am surprised by something I didn't expect or anticipate.

1 — 2 — 3 — 4 — 5 — 6 — 7 — 8 — 9 — 10

9. My friends and family would consider me to be risk-averse.

1 — 2 — 3 — 4 — 5 — 6 — 7 — 8 — 9 — 10

10. I believe that I am unsafe and that the world is a hostile place.

1 — 2 — 3 — 4 — 5 — 6 — 7 — 8 — 9 — 10

If you scored between 76 and 100, fear clutters your brain and rules over many choices that you make in your life. Don't be discouraged, for being aware of this fact, you can start to witness and eventually shift the role that fear plays in your life. Know that awareness is the first step towards healing. You can start by taking small steps. For example, ask to become aware of times when fear is rampant in your life. Pay attention to tightness in your shoulders, stomach, or other body parts. As you do, simply sit and have a dialogue with the fear. As you witness and commit to learning more about it, your relationship with it will change.

If you scored between 51 and 75, although fear does not completely run your life, it plays a significant role in cluttering your brain and keeping you stuck. Allow yourself to sit with fear when it arises, noting how strong it is, where you hold it in your body, and any diversions you use to avoid feeling it. Doing so will build your awareness of the role that fear plays in your life and will set you back on course as you practice compassion and loving-kindness towards yourself.

If you scored between 26 and 50, you have made great strides around working through your fears. A wise teacher once instructed me that my goal should not be to get rid of fear, but to act despite the fear. You need not remove fear from your life, but you do need to work with it. See it tucked away in a small corner of your brain. Eventually, as you become more awakened, trust will replace fear within your psyche, and the fear will melt away.

If you scored between 10 and 25, congratulations! Fear does not run your life. You make many choices from the place of love over fear, and your life reflects this. Make a commitment to seeing on a deeper level how fear still exists in your life. Once you do, you can uncover layers of fear that might surprise you. Know that they are tiny in comparison to the risks you are willing to take. Continue to stretch your comfort zone, knowing that in doing so, you cocreate for yourself a life of awe and adventure.

Getting Clear on Fear

Now that you have done the profile, you are more aware of the role that fear plays in your life, large or small. Here's a way of taking an inventory of your fears. You're going to need a piece of paper and a pen.

Take three breaths, releasing any tension in your body, and committing to opening your heart. Melt into yourself and surrender to any resistance.

Now ask your heart, *What fears am I not aware of? What fears am I avoiding in my life?* As the fears arise, write them down. When done, ask again, more pointedly, *What fears am I not aware of that are holding me back in my life . . . in relationship with myself, others, and my Creator?*

Are there any fears about my health? . . . Any fears about aging? . . . Any fears about incrimination from other people? . . . Fears about living my truth? . . . Fears of being mocked or judged by others?

Any fears about the world, the earth? . . . Any fears about religion or culture? . . . Any fears about my relationship with myself? . . . Fears about not living the life I am meant to live, about not being fulfilled?

Keep writing down any and all fears that arise.

Completing this exercise will open a portal of communication with your fears. You will likely continue to witness more ways in which fear takes charge in your life. As you do, list them. Simply observe them unconditionally.

The Depth of My Fear

For years, I kept thinking that I had to work on getting over my fears. I encourage you not to waste the time or make the effort to get rid of your fears. They exist, and your job is to take action despite them.

In fact, the more I watched my fears and asked for insights about them, the more I saw that I was constantly in fear about the smallest of things. I was shocked. For example, one day when I was working as a teacher's assistant at a local kindergarten class, the teacher asked me to place a flyer on each of the children's mail shelves. As I performed this mundane task, I started to notice a tightening of my abdomen. I felt a tightening of everything and watched the anxiety build within me. I allowed the thoughts to arise and witnesses them, "What if I miss one of the shelves? What if one of the children does not get his or her notice?" Wow! I was experiencing fear over a ridiculously simple task.

Then the other day, I was having a conversation with my dear friend Karen Lloyd. We were discussing all of the enterprises I was working on when she asked, "Theresa, with all that you do, are you ever afraid?"

It only took me a moment to consider a response: "Always. I am constantly in fear!"

I've come to realize that fear tears at me, from the smallest to the largest of tasks. While I can't speak for the rest of the world, I firmly believe that fear is part of the human condition. It is the greatest challenge that we face as humans. If we take disturbances down to their basest form, fear is at the root of all of our issues. We will always experience it, at least until we are enlightened and fully realized (while I am not, my understanding is that once you are enlightened, fear no longer has a hold on you). I'm not there yet, but I sure plan to be someday!

The good news is that we can note the fear and then keep moving forward despite it. This is how I work with fear. I first ask the Universe to reveal my fears to me. When I see fear arise within me, I do the following: I note it (trying to do so without judgment or condemnation); I pay attention to how it manifests in my body; I listen to its message (trying to remain neutral and neither ignore nor buy into it); then I feel the feelings that arise. If I want to cry, I cry. If I have an urge to laugh, I laugh. Whatever comes up, I stay with the feelings until they fully subside. Then I express gratitude for the lesson, and I take action: I keep on moving in the direction I intended.

There Are No Regrets When Action Is Taken

When I was young, people tried to dissuade me from leaving home to go to university, but I saw it as a wonderful adventure, and I went. It was difficult at times. I paid most of my way myself, but it was extraordinary. Those years in which I was living at the college were some of the best years of my life. Soon after graduating, I was discouraged from becoming an actor, but I decided to do it anyway. Again, no regrets. By the time I hit forty and felt ready to have a child, I could safely say that no stone had remained unturned. I had traveled the world, I had followed my dream career, and my life felt rich and full. I didn't feel that I sacrificed a life yet unlived for my daughter. My life was full of magical experiences, and I was ready and raring to start the next phase of my life.

You'll hear those fearful voices echoing in your mind. During those times that you apparently fail (when you do an audition and you don't get the part, for example), those critical, fearful voices in your head will be saying, "You were warned. You shouldn't be doing it."

Those voices will still be there, but we have to live despite them. Don't expect fear to go away. Don't expect anxiety to go away. It's about witnessing the fear, watching it, and then taking action nonetheless. I can honestly say that I have never regretted taking a risk of any kind. Even when the experience did not manifest the way I had planned, it always brought me one step closer to where I knew I was supposed to be.

Often we avoid our fear, and, like a wound, it starts to grow. It starts to get really ugly because we don't want to face it.

It really helped me to work with Dr. David Hawkins. He said that there's one thing that has been predetermined in our lives: the moment of our death. Some believe this, some don't. For me, this insight has reduced my fear. It has freed me from worry about getting into an accident or dying before my time was up (although I still look both ways when I cross the street). If the moment I'm going to die is predestined, what a relief! I don't have to worry about dying. This idea freed me from a sense of doom, from a sense that "if I do this, then I could cause that." If I get into the car, I can say, "It's already predetermined. I can let that one go." I was able to work through that fear just from that piece of knowledge from Dr. David Hawkins. Thank you, David.

Exercise 3: The Fear Flip

Here's one exercise to help you shift your fear. I find it really helpful. For this exercise, have a pen and paper handy.

Again, get comfortable. Take some deep breaths in and out. With each inbreath, see your heart opening wider and wider. With the outbreath, release any anxiety, any questions, relaxing deep, deep.

Contemplate the things that attract fearful thoughts within you. As you do, write each thought or potential circumstance down. Take your time and allow each to rise up within you. No need to dwell on them. As they appear, simply write them down and continue doing the slow, deep breathing.

Ask for guidance from the Universal Source. Set an intention that any fears that are blocking you arise. Once you find that no additional fears arise, go back to your list. Starting with the first fear, go through each of the fears listed and write the opposite of that. For example, if the fear is, "I fear that my child will die before me," then write in the affirmative and in the present tense, "My child is healthy and safe. She will outlive me and experience a long, joyful life." After writing the affirmation, take some time to imagine and feel into it. Seeing your child living a long and joyful life. Feel fully into experiencing them in a state of bliss and longevity. Once you feel complete, you can move on to the next fear on the list.

This exercise may take some time, so feel free to do what energizes you. You don't have to complete it all in one sitting. Go within and listen to your guidance. If your energy starts to wane, end the process and return to it at another time.

One of our greatest challenges is our resistance. With this exercise, you are acknowledging your fears and addressing them. However, you are not dwelling on them. You are reprogramming your brain to shift its perception. Do not underestimate the potency of this exercise.

When fears spontaneously arise in your mind, take a moment to do this exercise. State the opposite in an affirmative manner, and feel into it as if it were happening in the present moment.

Comparison Does Not Support Growth

Once a woman said to the Dalai Lama, "I've lost my son in war." She was devastated and grieved. With great compassion, he leaned over to her and said, "I lost an entire country." There's always someone who's experienced more pain.

On the other hand, be careful not to compare experiences. Another's pain, even if it is greater, doesn't take away your grief or pain. Be watchful of your own self-incrimination and judgment. I've seen people say, "This mother has lost a child. My child's only broken her arm. Who am I to be upset?" Don't go there. That's a form of resistance. Pain is not a point of competition, so someone else's pain should never dull yours or make it seem insignificant. Your pain is yours, so allow yourself that pain. Don't compare. Like the Dalai Lama, have great compassion for your pain and support yourself through it.

The Difference Between Expressing and Releasing

Sheila Zangar, a wonderful author and expert, has a technique for going into feeling. In the beginning, I struggled with Sheila, because I'd done a lot of cathartic work over the years—fully expressing my feelings, my anger—but her process was centered around experiencing rather than expressing emotions.

Sheila was wonderful in clarifying the difference for me. She said that expressing and releasing those feelings—say by banging a tennis racket against a pillow—was fine, but she pointed out that sometimes there's resistance in that too. She suggested going into what we were actually feeling without necessarily acting it out.

I still think there's merit in acting things out. Especially having history as an actor, I'm a passionate individual, and I have to do something with that energy, but that sense of going quietly within, surrendering to those feelings and allowing your body, mind and soul to fully feel them, can be extremely valuable too.

When you do the exercise, often you'll notice certain parts of the body tightening or tensing. That probably shows where you're holding that anxiety or fear or anger. Be in that place in the body. In later chapters, I'll describe some exercises for healing by listening to the body as it speaks to us.

Melting and Opening Resistance

You might find that after this exercise, fears start to show up in your dreams (or you can be walking around, and oops, there's another one). You've opened the portal to exploring these fears, and now that you've welcomed them into your life to be healed, they'll start showing up for you, perhaps at odd times and in odd places.

Have a pencil and paper handy. Just write those fears down. Then go through the exercise of experiencing them completely, surrendering to them, and seeing where they take you and how they may or may not melt away.

It might take several experiences to complete this process. You might see resistance showing up. You might hit walls and say, "I can't go any further with this. This is too painful." Honor that, accept it, don't judge it, don't fear it, and then try again.

Personally, I have a great fear that I will not live my soul's journey to its full expanse—that I'll fail to do what I was brought here to do. Another fear is that my life has been a lie and that my spiritual endeavors are a farce—the fear that I am a phony, fooling myself and others about any altruistic efforts I have made in my life.

I've also had fears around my daughter. I endured that car crash when I was three months pregnant with her, and I had radiation and lots of CAT scans, MRIs, and X-rays throughout the pregnancy, because I'd broken bones on my spine. Three months after the crash, I'd hear the radiation technologists whisper, "She's six months pregnant. We can't do this. But the doctor says we have to." I'd made them cover me threefold with those lead bibs. I had a lot of anxiety about whether my daughter was going to come out a green, glowing, radioactive little being. She was born in perfect health.

A Moment in Time

When I arrived at my favorite coffee shop (Peet's in Downers Grove, Illinois), I turned on my computer, ready to start writing again. However, when I opened my laptop, the first things that popped up was an invitation to the Ekam World Peace Festival to End All War (theme: global harmony). It was starting just as I clicked on the "Join us" tab (a sign from the Universe, so I let go of my agenda and followed it).

The first contemplation in the festival focused on the horrible fires in the Amazon rainforest. The teacher spoke of man's greed and selfishness as the cause of such destructive forces. "What happens to one here affects all the rest. One individual can shift the energy of generations to come . . . as you contribute with your noble hearts . . . and bless all individuals in pain."

My eyes welled up with tears as I got in touch with the pain that rests deep inside me. While it was tough in a crowded café, I allowed the tears to come. Unlike in the past, I no longer try to analyze why, because this is a distraction from being present with my feelings.

I was then reminded of an incident the previous night. I was in the right-turn lane, and there was a car in front of me. The driver had many opportunities to turn but did not. Type-A Theresa started honking. Once the light changed and we turned, I raced past him, cursing him all the while. At the next stoplight, he pulled up beside me. I asked him why he didn't turn. He remained calm and explained that there was a no-right-turn sign at that intersection, and that he had been stopped by the police in the past.

I apologized profusely, and we went on our way. In such situations in the past, there would have been a yelling match between us, but not this time. I was in a different place. I was immediately humbled by my error and my impatience. If the outer world reflects our inner state of being, then I was graced with a shift. I was filled with deep gratitude and humility. What an extraordinary gift!

Once we are aware of the wars that are raging within us, our greatest challenge (or opportunity) is to give ourselves and our misguided anger the acceptance and love that we would an innocent young child, for we are all children, doing our best to navigate our way around the playground of life.

When she was young, my daughter was the most fearless being I had ever met. She'd be balancing on the beams at the playground, she'd be climbing trees, and I'd be thinking, "Oh, God."

I found myself paralyzed by fear, but I didn't want her to feel it and start reacting to it. When I was a child, I could feel my mother's anxieties around things like waiting for a train, walking at the mall or getting on elevators. We'd have to stand right beside each other; we'd be right up against the wall. Now let's be clear: she was an incredible mother. Caring for four daughters that were born within six years was not easy. I know that her precautions were absolutely necessary. However, not only did I internalize those fears, but I intensified them. Subsequently, I didn't want my over-zealous fears to be internalized by my daughter. So, while I would not let her be reckless, when I noted my fears taking over, I would set an intention and request, "Angels, take care of her." I would hand it right over to them and say to myself, "I'm going to let go and trust that they are taking care of her."

This freed up the energy I was losing over worrying for her. Again, it's a matter of conviction. I absolutely believed that when I called those angels in, they were there, and they were taking care of her. I called the angels about three minutes before my car crashed. Several spiritual masters told me that I had a massive team of angels there supporting me. To this day, I know they were there.

During one of our conversations, author and spiritual teacher Sonia Choquette said to me, "We all have these wonderful angels, but we forget to ask them for help. They're hanging around waiting for us, so it's as simple as going, 'Hey, guys, I need help here.'"

Similarly, with the worry and anxiety about my daughter, I simply say, "Angels, take care of her." Boom. The fear is gone, and I'm relieved.

Step 2

Commit to Inner Integrity

The second, and perhaps the most difficult, step you need to commit to is inner integrity. When I learned more about this step, I was both shocked and delighted. I was attending the Deepening Process in India, when our teacher, Bhagavan, shared the following story:

One of his followers was an extremely successful and renowned heart surgeon. He had been studying with Bhagavan for quite some time and was a diligent student. One day he had a patient on his operating table. The patient, a young man, was not faring well. In the midst of the surgery, his heart stopped beating. Immediately the surgeon began to pray to his Divine, asking that the patient be spared. He prayed and prayed, "Sweet Divine, this man is young and has a full life ahead of him. Please give him more time to live it out."

Despite his efforts, there was no change. So he called again upon his Divine: "Benevolent Creator, this man has a family, young children who will suffer great loss without their father. Please save him." Again, there was no change in the patient's condition. Then the surgeon remembered his master's teachings about inner authenticity. He prayed one last time, "Dear Sweet Divine, I desperately want this man to survive and heal completely. The truth is that my reputation as a top surgeon is very important to me. I fear for myself. I want him to be healed for my own personal gains." Immediately the man's heart started to beat again, and ultimately the surgery was a great success.

This story is a powerful example of inner integrity. Once the surgeon became brutally honest and searched within himself, he realized that his prayers were for his own self-serving needs to be met. Once he realized this and faced the truth of his motives and became honest with both himself and his Divine, energetic obstacles were cleared, and the tide turned.

When I first considered this, I chuckled to myself. It was both liberating and somewhat uncomfortable to realize that I cannot fool myself, or the Universe. While I may attempt to, I know the truth in my heart and soul, as does my Creator.

The first step you need to take is to make a heartfelt commitment to living in integrity. In my opinion, inner integrity involves looking very deeply at our motivations, actions, and intentions. As I contemplate them, I have found that they are not always pretty. Often they are quite narcissistic, selfish, and downright ugly. As

I say, "It sucks being human, but we each chose to be in this lifetime!"

Before we go any further, take some time to honor yourself and move forward on your commitment to decluttering your brain by reflecting and doing your own inner integrity profile.

Inner Integrity Profile

While we are all aware of integrity and the role it plays in the world, committing to inner integrity takes you to a much deeper place. At times, you may be unaware of how much you fool and manipulate yourself. A great indication of a lack of inner integrity comes in adamant or defensive responses. That old saying "Thou dost protest too much" speaks volumes. For each of the questions below, take care to pause and ask your deepest self for the truth. Then choose the number that is most closely aligns to your situation (1 being "not at all" and 10 being "a great deal").

1. Do you believe that you are deceptive with yourself?
1 — 2 — 3 — 4 — 5 — 6 — 7 — 8 — 9 — 10

2. Do you ever catch yourself exaggerating and then trying to cover it up?
1 — 2 — 3 — 4 — 5 — 6 — 7 — 8 — 9 — 10

3. Are you defensive in nature?
1 — 2 — 3 — 4 — 5 — 6 — 7 — 8 — 9 — 10

4. Do you find it difficult to keep secrets when asked?
1 — 2 — 3 — 4 — 5 — 6 — 7 — 8 — 9 — 10

5. Do you tend to lie about your weight, height, or age?
1 — 2 — 3 — 4 — 5 — 6 — 7 — 8 — 9 — 10

6. Do you feel disappointed in yourself when you stretch the truth?
1 — 2 — 3 — 4 — 5 — 6 — 7 — 8 — 9 — 10

7. Do you catch yourself manipulating others?
1 — 2 — 3 — 4 — 5 — 6 — 7 — 8 — 9 — 10

8. Do you find that you cheat, even in little ways?
1 — 2 — 3 — 4 — 5 — 6 — 7 — 8 — 9 — 10

9. If you are given too much change, do you return it?
1 — 2 — 3 — 4 — 5 — 6 — 7 — 8 — 9 — 10

10. Do you avoid righting your wrongs and apologizing when in error?
1 — 2 — 3 — 4 — 5 — 6 — 7 — 8 — 9 — 10

If you scored between 76 and 100, you have a great deal to explore in the area of your inner integrity. See this not as condemnation, but as a sign that you are on the right path and are moving in the right direction. If you are struggling in seeing how you are wanting in inner integrity, practice opening your heart and ask your higher self to reveal this to you. Note the times when you are defensive within yourself, or with others. Often defensiveness is a sign that you are uncomfortable looking at something within yourself. Avoid defending your defensiveness. Get still and look within for the answers.

If you scored between 51 and 75, you have taken some steps towards inner integrity. Continue on your journey of self-discovery, knowing that at times it can be a tough pill to swallow. Seeing ourselves for who we are—the good, the bad, and the ugly—can be daunting, so it is important to treat the errors of your ways as you would treat a child who has gone off course. Choose to express compassion and encourage deeper honesty in the future. When you do, you will prevent yourself from experiencing further shame and blame clutter in your brain.

If you scored between 26 and 50, you have made vast strides in your commitment to be in integrity from the inside out. Once you ask the Universe to reveal to you where you are not in integrity, you will receive additional messages that will assist you in further aligning yourself. Be sure to note without judgment when you are not in integrity. Witness this truth and allow it to inform the present and direct the future.

If you scored between 10 and 25, you are very good at being honest with yourself. For the most part, you are committed to living your life with inner integrity. The more you commit, the more you will find yourself out of alignment in ways that you didn't previously realize. Be gentle with yourself when you do, and credit yourself for how far you have come. Know in your heart that committing to inner integrity is one of the most self-fulfilling things you could do.

It Can Be Tricky to See When We Are Lying to Ourselves

How did you do? Were any surprises revealed to you? If you haven't yet received any "aha" insights, I assure you, you will. As you deeply commit to looking authentically at yourself, you will find that the Universe orchestrates many situations that will support you in seeing, experiencing, and healing on deeper and deeper levels. The highest part of you wants decluttering and greater peace of mind. It is your birthright and privilege. As you continue to practice these steps, you will find that you no longer need to stew about the hows and whys; you are able to note them, feel into them, and then move on. Your brain is no longer cluttered with the bantering that was weighing upon your conscience and zapping your energy.

Being brutally honest with myself around my own inauthenticity has been eye-opening. I know that I am a work in progress. I recently dragged my seventeen-year old daughter to a consciousness-raising workshop. Like all teens, she had her issues, and I wanted to help ease the burdens and stressors in her life. She is a beautiful soul, and deserves an easy, joyful life.

At least that's what I told myself, but as she slept throughout the first several hours, I felt my blood starting to boil. That crazy voice in my head began to take over the calm that I was "efforting" during the meditations.

As I continued to meditate and contemplate the feelings that were arising, it became crystal-clear that as I dug deeper, the angst was all about *me*. Yes, I love my daughter, and yes, I want her to have faith in being supported by a higher consciousness, but I realized that underneath the apparent altruistic mothering, my motivations were selfish. I wanted to feel like a good mother. I wanted my life to be easier, and if she struggled less, so would I.

Once I realized this, while tempted to judge the heck out of myself, I giggled at the realization. I felt liberated and somewhat proud of owning the truth. I laughed at the lightness that resulted from my self-confession, and I forged ahead, able to continue the workshop, peeling away additional layers of self-uncovery.

Now let's take a further look at the mind traps you have likely developed around inner integrity.

Inauthentic Altruism

Sometimes authenticity comes from a place of *should* and *should not* rather than being rooted in what I desire and what I think is right. I always prided myself in being selfless and giving to others—being somebody who goes beyond the call of duty. When I delved deeper into this, I started noting that I felt anxious and unappreciated.

When I delved even further and my witness-self was observing, I noted that I wasn't doing these things because I wanted to in my heart. I was doing them to please others, to be loved. I realized that at my core, I was not feeling that I myself was enough, and many of my "selfless" acts were in fact coming from this wounded place. Many tears were shed over this realization. It was painful to see and difficult to overcome. Then, as the Universe so wonderfully does, I was given a gift to further this understanding.

A Gift from Oprah

Several years ago, Oprah Winfrey was no longer doing her daily television show, but she was still recording webcasts in her Chicago studio. I responded to a survey on her website, and I was invited to ask questions at one of her webinars. It was magical to be backstage getting hair and makeup done. I was thrilled.

Oprah's guest was author Iyanla Vanzant. I was enthusiastic, as I had written a study guide for one of Iyanla's books several years prior. I loved her work. At one point near the end of the program, Iyanla asked Oprah, "What has been your greatest spiritual challenge?"

Oprah responded that her most difficult trial was in people's expectations—their sense of entitlement to her, her fame, and her money. "Not my sense of entitlement," she said, "but more other people's sense of entitlement."

I then asked, "What did you do about this? Because I'm experiencing other people's sense of entitlement and their lack of appreciation for what I do."

Oprah's response was life-altering. She stopped giving to friends and family for a while. She decided to give only when she wanted to and when it made her feel good. Only then would she give.

At that point in the conversation, I shared that I was going through something similar in my life. I was doing a lot of volunteering. I was spreading myself too thin, trying to make special cakes, trying to help out friends. I was running all the social events for my community. I was on the board of directors for my neighborhood, I was doing a lot of volunteering for Toastmasters. I was pushing myself too far, and then resenting it, believing that nobody really appreciated me.

"Wait a second, Theresa," Oprah said. "*Who* doesn't appreciate you? Do *you* appreciate you?"

When I started investigating, I realized that I was not being authentic with myself. I was not appreciating myself, and I was burning myself out. I needed people to think that I was Superwoman. I had the belief that maybe if I was extraordinary, others would then love and honor me. This of course was rooted in the belief that if I were simply me, then I would not be enough.

Oprah's advice was not to give until I really wanted to, but because it made me feel good, because doing so would come from my heart, not from a place of neediness. So for a while I stopped giving.

I stopped volunteering for my community, I left the board of directors and stopped bringing home-baked goods to school activities. When Oprah called me on my wounded sense of self, I realized that I had been overcontributing with edginess. I did not believe that I deserved to have more free time. I didn't think I had a right to say no. I feared that if I said no, others would not love me.

It was interesting to watch it all progress. For several years, I had run all of the social events in my community, and I worked hard at them. I stopped doing so, and a couple of people took over. The first thing they said was, "How did you manage all of this by yourself?" Then I received compliments from some of the kids: "It's not like it used to be, Ms. Puskar. What happened? We want you back." It wasn't until I left it behind and took care of myself that I felt appreciated, but I knew that the block was my own lack of appreciation for my efforts. While families likely shared their appreciation, I couldn't hear them. I was too busy "doing"!

When I pulled back, I saw my contributions and started honoring myself. I realized that whatever my motivation was, I did a pretty darn good job. In pulling back and being authentic with myself, I was starting to get the appreciation that only came after I started to appreciate myself. The outside world mirrors what's going on inside of us. If we don't appreciate ourselves, we cannot expect others to do so. I have since given up many of those activities, and in doing so, I have freed up a lot more time for self-care.

Saying No with an Open Heart

One lesson I learned about saying no has been invaluable. Again, it came from doing the inner work—honest self-assessment. I noted that when I first said no to requests of my time, I did so with an edginess. There was a defensiveness and anger in my tone. As I allowed myself to feel into the anger and explore it, I realized that it was rooted in the belief that I did not deserve time for myself. I believed that I did not have the right to say no, and if I did, I was unlovable.

Once I noted this, I started a new dialogue with my inner voice. I worked on convincing that part of me that never felt enough that I *was* enough. That simply by choosing to live on this earth at this time, I was enough. I did not need to do anything extraordinary.

This is still a work in progress. However, I am finding that the more confidence I have in myself, the more I am able to say no to others with an open heart and a gentle disposition. The angry response to the request was defensive, because in my heart of hearts, I didn't believe I had the right to say no.

If you start to withdraw from your overachieving in angst and edginess—"I'm not doing this anymore. You people don't appreciate me"—be gentle with yourself. That's the little person inside you saying, "I did this really beautiful coloring, and nobody sees it." Be kind and compassionate, as the Divine is with you, and tell the struggling child within your subconscious that she is safe and lovable just the way she is. She needs to do nothing in order to be loved. She has been lovable since the moment of her birth, and she needs to do nothing to prove herself.

Make a commitment to love your edginess, seeing it as defensiveness, but also as a first step towards opening your heart and honoring yourself. Note where the defensiveness comes from, and then accept it. In time, you will learn to say no to others gently and with an open heart.

Exercise 4: Energy Drain or Gain Check-in

Get a pen and a paper and create a list of all of the things you do for others. They can be very small, like feeding the neighbors' cat when they're on vacation, or very big, like serving on a board of directors, running an event at your child's school, or being part of the office social committee. Also, make note of tasks you do for others for which you should be financially compensated.

Once you've completed that list, take some deep breaths. Relax and allow yourself to let go and be present. Go back to your ten-year-old self. Imagine your heart opening. Find that joy in your heart.

Go back to the list, look at each entry, and ask yourself, "Does this bring me joy? Am I doing this for *me*, or am I doing it because I believe I have to in order to be lovable? Does this energize me, or does it actually take energy from me?"

If you find that this activity feeds you energetically and brings you joy, put a check mark beside it. It's good for you. In doing it, you are being authentic with yourself. You will not suffer, and you will go forward in your life.

If, however, you find it depletes you and doesn't bring you joy, put an X beside it. Consider letting it go. Start allowing yourself to say no. You will free up time to nurture and care for yourself.

What little things can you start to do for yourself? Make a commitment to practice some self-care, even for five minutes a day. You could start a doodle art project, take a hot therapeutic bath, or simply sit and acknowledge yourself for all of the goodness that you bring to the world. As you practice this, your life will expand and you will have more free time, which will create an energetic vacuum that allows other wonders to appear in your life.

You Deserve Compensation

Recently I became aware of how much work I was doing for others without being financially compensated. The benevolent Universe stepped in again, in the form of a mentor. I was writing my monthly article for *Conscious Community* magazine, and the gentleman I was interviewing offered to coach me pro bono. His first directive was to stop working for others without being financially compensated. This was very difficult for me, as I was extremely uncomfortable talking dollars and cents and negotiating contracts.

The first individual I confronted became very angry and accused me of abandoning her halfway through her project. While I wanted to defend myself and counter her attack with rhetoric about her own abandonment issues, I chose the high road and said nothing. It was difficult, though!

Within a week, another woman asked me to do some work without being paid. I politely told her (without explanation or excuses) that I could not. Her response was very different. She said that she absolutely understood and felt privileged that I was even having a conversation with her, given my history and expertise. She said that she would pray on finding a way to create a win-win situation, and she did.

Here we have two examples in which I committed first and foremost to myself. What was exciting was that I didn't have the edginess. I spoke about how I needed to respect and honor myself more, without attacking the other for their request. This was a sign that I'm actually getting to the point of feeling that I deserve, that I am good enough.

Transition Can Take Time

Don't expect things to turn around immediately. While they may, sometimes such huge transitions take time. After all, we have been living with our previous patterning for many years.

Some advice about edginess: first of all, be careful about sending emails or letters. I've learned in the past that I can be quite upset with somebody, type away on the computer, press *send*, and then think, "Oh my God, what have I done?" Initial responses can often be reactionary and caustic. Because you are not expressing one-to-one, heart-to-heart, your refusals can be misconstrued.

I recommend saving your email as a draft and giving yourself time to ponder it. With sensitive matters, I often call the individual or meet with him/her, with a commitment to keeping my heart open, honoring both myself and the other person while taking a stand to support myself.

What was key for me, though, was loving the edgy part of myself. It takes a lot to forgive yourself for that edginess and see it as a sign: "Thank you, edginess. You're my buddy. I appreciate you. You're a part of me, and you're giving me the message that something is not working here for me."

It's a matter of honoring that edginess, having a dialogue with it, and forgiving yourself. For years, I would lash out and afterward hate who I was. While the others didn't like what I did, they went on with their lives. They were done with it, but I was constantly beating myself up for what I did.

Anger is a behavior. It is not who you are. Yes, it's a choice you make. It is a response, very often a reactive one. In that case, you might realize that you are in reaction mode. You are being triggered, and there is some issue within you that you need to address. You need the courage to look within and say, "If I'm triggered, it's about me and my relationship to *me*. Let's look at this. Why am I upset? Why did I get so angry when they asked me to do one more party? Why am

I not feeling appreciated? Because I'm exhausted, because I'm overburdening myself, and because I keep thinking I'm not enough."

Start looking at what is going on inside you, in your relationship with yourself. Have compassion, be honest and reflective with yourself, and start noting the reactivity. Take a couple of breaths, root yourself and the other in love, and then commit to keeping your heart open. If you notice that the reactivity comes from your judgment of yourself, give yourself a blast of love. Give the little girl inside a big hug.

Being authentic isn't always pretty, but being inauthentic is downright ugly. Remember that and live by that, and you will stop suffering and begin to start living in your life.

Aggressively Denying That You Are Passive-Aggressive

One of the traits in others that most annoyed me was passive-aggressiveness. I abhorred it, claiming that "With me, you know what you get. I'm downright aggressive. No phoniness, no pretense, no subtle manipulation or passive-aggressiveness."

However, as I committed to greater clarity and asked for opportunities to see what I was uncomfortable seeing in myself, I was alarmed to see just how manipulative I was and how much I was aggressively denying my own passive-aggressiveness. (Some of these are real tongue twisters. If they do that to your tongue, you can imagine what they do to our minds.)

Something to note: When you are triggered and adamant about something you despise in others, look within. Either you're acting it out or you behave in the opposite extreme. Either way, you are reacting to your fear about having that trait. In other words, if you adamantly say, "That's not in me," it probably means that you've totally disowned it and you've gone to the opposite extreme. You have to be honest with yourself and look at where it is in you. It can be very tricky.

Not long ago I was taking the train to work. It was stormy and snowy, and the train was very full. I saw a young, beautiful blonde girl turn one of the seats over so she had it facing her and no one could sit in it. She proceeded to put her wet, dirty boots on the seat.

The judgmental, Goody-Two-shoes voice inside me thought, "She's misbehaving. She's being rude and disrespectful, and she shouldn't be allowed to get away with it."

The conductor came around and said, "Please be respectful of everyone else on the train and keep your shoes or boots off the seat in front of you. Allow seats for everyone." She ignored his request and kept her boots on the seat. Seeing all these people standing on the train while her boots were on that seat, I started to feel anger building inside of me. I had a daydream about moving her boots, taking a Kleenex, wiping off the seat, and throwing the Kleenex on her lap.

Then I thought, "We'll see what happens when the conductor comes by again to collect her ticket. Is she going to leave her boots on the seat? I don't think so."

Sure enough, the conductor came by, and she took her boots off the seat for him and put them back on after he left.

By the end of the trip my witness-self was saying, "Theresa, do you see how worked up you're getting? She's fine over there in her own little world." I watched the energy inside me start to bubble up. I watched the tightening of my muscles. I noted the tension in my stomach, and I became aware of how much energy I lost in my angry inner tirade. I was reacting to her passive-aggressiveness, and I wanted to get aggressive about it. It triggered a part in me that would like to break the rules, that would like to put my feet on the chair, although I was never allowed to.

I think I was jealous because as a child, I always wanted to be defiant, but I never would let myself. I didn't want to step out of place at all. There was a little girl inside me who, from a very young age, would not break the rules. She had to be perfect, and if she stepped out of line, she considered herself a failure.

If I Step out of Line, I Am Not Lovable

I remember one day when my sister was called up to the wall at school. I was horrified! She broke the rules. As she stood there, in front of the entire school, she started giggling, laughing, and waving to her friends. I thought to myself, "Wow, I wish I'd let myself do that." There was my passive-aggressiveness.

My experience on the train taught me that I have to let go. People make their mistakes. They have their own agendas. Perhaps there was a little girl in her psyche that was suffering, a little girl who was constantly beaten and told that she was dirt. That wounded child might have been saying to herself, "I'm going to stand up for myself now. I am going to be defiant, and my boots will stay where they are."

It was interesting to have my witness-self watching me get all worked up, then realizing how much energy I was depleting in my reactivity. I had to first have compassion and love for myself for the part of me that felt like a little reactive child who wanted to be bad and wasn't allowed to. Then and only then could I feel more compassion for the girl, letting my judgment melt away. Then the thoughts turned to, "I don't know her or her situation. I am labeling her as defiant, but what do I know? In the whole scheme of my life, what does it really matter?"

To this day, I still see her, and I watch her get on the train. I wonder if she's still acting defiantly, but now I'm aware that the issue rests with me, not her.

Calling Out My Passive-Aggressive Behavior

Since I've asked to become more aware of my own passive-aggressive behavior, I catch myself doing things. If someone is not walking fast enough on the train platform, I'll move into their body space, as if to energetically say, "Move on, pal, I have somewhere to go." I often find myself doing this, even when there is nowhere to go and nothing to do. As I reflect on my incessant sense of urgency, I can feel angst well up inside of me. Where is it rooted? I discovered that it is rooted in my fear of not meeting my life goals before I die. Sounds crazy, but if you find yourself constantly rushing from one task to the next, you might ask yourself what the underlying reason might be. As you peel away the layers, you most often find fear at the root of your anxiety.

Shifting Aggression through a Sense of Deserving

One particular person in my life was extremely passive-aggressive, and I judged him harshly. Now he is a gift who shows me my own passive-aggressive tendencies. When I start to judge him, the inner dialogue has shifted to, "Wow, Theresa, you have passive-aggressiveness in you. You're not exempt from it, and that's why you judge him." It helps to see myself soften around his passive-aggressiveness and to see him being aware of and softening around mine.

Is it better to be aggressive or passive-aggressive? That is the million-dollar question. Sometimes I just have to be aware of it and say, "I was just downright aggressive." I'm really working on my aggressiveness, because I'm finding it self-defeating, and it's one of the best ways I have to beat myself up.

If we really believe we have a right to something, we don't act aggressively. I've seen some stand confidently and say, "I'm sorry. That doesn't work for me" in a way that is gentle. Their hearts are open and loving. They speak their truth and create healthy boundaries. The other person responds with acceptance and appreciation. As I observe this, I think, "If I asked for the same thing, we'd be butting heads." Why? Because deep in my heart, I don't really believe I deserve to ask for it.

If you find yourself being aggressive, it's a clue that you don't really believe you deserve something. If you find yourself being passive-aggressive, it's probably the same thing, but in addition, you don't believe you have the option to speak, so you behave in roundabout ways, in ways that are not forthright. You might think, "Let's accidentally bump her purse. Oops. Sorry."

Exercise 5: Examining Your Passive-Aggressive Tendencies

One approach is to go to your Highest Self and ask, "Am I passive-aggressive? If I am, please show me how." You might choose to do this before you go to bed, or first thing in the morning.

Another fun exercise you could try is to send yourself, or someone else, a love bomb. For example, the next time I see that girl on the train, instead of going into judgment, I could imagine sending a blast of beautiful white or golden light to her. But I also need to see that light growing from my heart and filling me, because my judgment of her is a reflection of my judgment of myself.

In the beginning, the love bomb might not feel right. It might even feel phony. It might feel as if it's not rooted in love. Send it anyway.

When you notice that you're judging other people, when you're noticing passive-aggressiveness or aggressiveness in others, and you're starting to feel reactive, see this loving light filling your heart and theirs.

And remember this: when someone is pushing your buttons, those are *your* buttons. They are not actually doing the pushing: *you* are. If you are like me, you may find yourself shocked at the myriad ways in which you have stretched the truth, lying to yourself and to your Divine.

Letting Yourself Lose at Losing

I have always tried to cultivate noncompetitiveness within myself, and for the most part, I believed that I was not a competitive person. As I watched others around me who were highly competitive, I would shrug my shoulders and tell myself that, unlike them, I didn't mind losing.

As I explored this aspect of myself more with the intention of inner integrity, I realized that I was fooling myself and that I was highly competitive. In truth, I hate losing! Once I realized this, as I tried to cultivate a comfort with losing, I learned that I was losing at allowing myself to lose.

Comparing Creativity: A Losing Battle

When I was a little girl, I was very creative. I won a competition among my schoolmates to take a class with a professional artist for a day. Within each of the schools in the Toronto area, they had chosen one or two children to work with this artist, and I was one of them. I was very excited!

I went to the class. I was probably around ten or eleven years old. One of the exercises we were given was to draw a baseball and a glove. When I was drawing, I was in bliss. Then I looked at the rendering that was being done by another little girl, who was also from my school, and I was devastated. Her drawing was exceptional. At that moment, the negative, competitive self-talk took over, and from that day forward, I never saw myself as an artist.

Nobody was there to teach me that each rendering is a soul creation; none is better or worse. I wish somebody had shown me Picasso's sculptures, Andy Warhol's paintings, or J. M. W. Turner's exquisite landscapes. They are all different and unique. But nobody in that class taught me that it's not about doing the drawing that has the closest resemblance to an actual baseball and glove; it's about the way I see, perceive, and express it that makes it precious.

A gift always comes with every loss. Years later, I remembered that experience when I was writing my children's books. I got excited about using that story to teach children to honor their creativity. I've now written a book, *Celebrate All You Create*, encouraging children to avoid competitiveness and appreciate their own creative expressions.

Sing Your Soul Song

There have been other times when I've thwarted my passion. I really love to sing; I always have. I studied voice throughout high school and university. I eventually started to get the leads in musicals, and my endeavors as a singer started to soar.

Then, as a professional actress, I began to audition for musicals. I noted that something peculiar started to happen. The more I studied, the more critical I became of my voice. As I'd start to sing, I would note a point at which my voice was not perfectly pitched, and I would cringe. Instead of focusing on the ninety-nine notes that were right, I would focus on that one poor note, and I would fall apart. In contrast, I had a friend who was not a singer; she was a character actress. I would watch her at these auditions; she would sing horribly, but with her all of her heart and soul. Ultimately, she got the professional jobs in the musicals.

Losing became a central part of my psyche. I'd grab those self-criticizing thoughts from the thought-mosphere and hold tightly on to them. Do you ever catch yourself doing so? I might get ninety-nine positive responses to a speaking-event survey or four stars for a performance. Yet what do I focus on? What keeps running through my mind? That one criticism, or that one star that I did not get. Does this sound familiar?

Thoughts start cluttering your brain, like "Maybe they're right. Maybe I am not enough. Maybe I should change my performance." You negate the ninety-nine percent of comments that were positive. Thus our tendency to be very hard on ourselves can move us towards losing.

Beyond Competitiveness

I've also had to work with my competitiveness as an actress. Acting is a highly competitive business. You have a couple of seconds to impress the decision makers at the beginning of an audition. You state your name and the agency that represents you, and if they don't see charisma, they are on to the next actor.

When I coach actors, I encourage them to compete only with themselves. Acting is such a goofy profession. It can be about the size of your nose or the color of your eyes. Especially in film and television, you have no control over what they're looking for. If you allow yourself to say, "I am a victim of their choosing process," you will never succeed. You have to go within and ask, "Did I do a good performance?" When I started focusing on "Did I do my best for myself?" while forgetting who else was out there, things started to shift. I started to feel better about myself, and I gave better performances.

Our culture perpetuates competitiveness, so it's a matter of choosing. Wayne Dyer did a great program called, "What Do You Really Want for Your Children?" It encouraged keeping children out of competitive sports, public schools, or anything that is based on competition. I listened to the program when my daughter was very young, and I planned on keeping her away at least from competitive sports. My husband, who was very involved in competitive sports, was not of that mind-set.

As time went on, my daughter wanted to be part of the softball team, and she wanted to play basketball. I realized that I can't compete with the competitive world out there. All I can do is try to arm her with an inner sense of who she is. It's very tricky. I still don't have all the answers, but I'm optimistic that she will keep things in perspective by listening to her own inner guides.

From Victim to Victor

I really shifted when I embraced the idea that I'm not a victim of anyone or anything. I am a product of my own beliefs and experiences. I was being considered for a role in *The X-Files*, and I got it. About six months later, I had an audition for a guest-starring role on the show. It was a wonderful opportunity for me. I diligently rehearsed the scene, and I was invited to a callback audition. I performed well and was invited to a third callback. Chris Carter, the creator, was there. It was the big finale.

I asked the actor I was to audition with if we could practice together. Once I heard his rendition of his role, I decided to change mine. I made entirely different character choices.

After that audition, the casting director approached me and said, "Theresa, what did you do? You totally changed your read. We called you back because what you had established was perfect in combination with the actor with whom you were reading."

I realized that I had questioned my inner guidance. I noticed that at that caliber of acting, the actors behave differently. They have a sense of calm and ease. They aren't practicing; they're chatting and talking with one another, laughing. A totally different energy. They have no apparent anxiety and have a real sense of who they are. Whereas actors auditioning for the smaller roles tend to be more tense, and somewhat frantic.

Exercise 6: Losing Intentionally

Within the next several days, I encourage you to allow yourself to lose intentionally. Let yourself lose at cards, or be the last in the turkey dinner line. Explore losing as your chief aim, as opposed to winning.

Do you feel more or less anxious when you do so? Do you feel pride, or do you feel anger rising up within you? Take some time to write about your experience. Note your feelings as you continue to explore any sense of urgency you might possess. I know that when I started reflecting, I was so competitive that I would catch myself trying to be the first in line to get on the train for work. I'd catch myself having to be first at everything and having to be the best at everything.

Overcoming this tendency can be very difficult, but it's something I really have to grapple with. If I don't, I could burn out my adrenal system by acting from a constant physical and mental state of fight-or-flight.

Exercise 7: Letting Go of Judgment

Here's another exercise I would encourage you to try. Take three deep breaths. As you breathe in, see light filling your body. As you breathe out, see any stress, tension, or negativity leaving your mind and body. Then breathe deeply into your heart, and see the light at the center of your heart expanding and growing as you breathe in, and expanding outward on your out-breath.

Think of an area of your life in which you really hate to lose. Breathe into that competitive place. Welcome that part of yourself. Then witness the judgments you express around your disdain for losing. How do you feel about that?

Then repeat to yourself, "I'm a conscious, evolved soul. I am loving and lovable. I hate that I don't like losing at this." Breathe and watch those judgments of yourself arise. Take note of where those judgments might be stored in your body. Feel if you are experiencing any tightness anywhere. If so, breathe through it.

Now imagine yourself at the age of five. You're in the schoolyard, and you are upset about losing. Then become the parent of this child. She comes to you in tears and says, "I'm losing. I don't like losing." What do you do?

As a loving parent, you hold her, wrap your arms around her, accept her completely, and explain to her that there will always be losing and winning in life.

Remind your child self that she needs to love herself even when losing.

Say to that child, "We're going to send loving light to you—beautiful, radiant white light. It's OK to lose, and it's OK not to like yourself because you're losing. Allow yourself those feelings. It's OK, beautiful. No need to worry."

Watch any judgments that come up around losing, especially those that say you are too evolved to get upset about losing. Send those judgments away. You might imagine yourself burying them in the ground or sending them to Archangel Michael to transform. In whatever way you feel comfortable, allow them to leave you. See your judgments as gifts and offer them to the Creative Source.

Keep breathing, allowing your body to feel calm, at ease, and at peace. When you feel ready, open your eyes and write about your experience.

A Loss Can Be a Step Forward

Losing is a state of mind. If you feel you're losing, honor that, but choose to move forward. Choose to know that losing might be a fleeting moment.

I remember hearing that Einstein failed the second grade. The world's greatest pioneers, intellects, scientists, and innovators lost more than they ever won. All of your victories are in waiting, and any loss means you're one step closer to experiencing the victory that you're looking for. See the loss as a step forward, and keep walking. You lose when you let winning and losing define who you are. You win when you allow losing to be part of your life experience, *without giving it permission to run the show.*

That's the difference. While winning and losing may be a part of life, you don't have to let them run the show.

To sum up, losing is comparing ourselves with what is outside of ourselves. If we go into our inner bliss and really work on what brings us joy, the energy shifts. Totally.

It's the same in the spiritual world: we put so many gurus and so many people above us. I think that's part of the loser mentality: Somebody else knows better. Somebody else has a better phone line to God. They're connected, but I have to be put on hold, and sometimes I get cut off.

We put spiritual teachers, actors, Hollywood stars, and those we deem "successful" on pedestals. As soon as we do, they are doomed, because eventually their humanness is going to reveal itself. When it does, they will fall very far, because they have been up so high.

Oprah Winfrey once said something to the effect of, "Get a life, people. If you had a really full life, you wouldn't dwell on the actors in Hollywood, who's loving whom, who's dating whom, or who's falling down."

If the outer world is a mirror or reflection of what's going on inside, all this means that we're not allowing ourselves to be human. We're not allowing ourselves to make mistakes, and we're stopping ourselves from the great messages that we have to offer, because we're saying, "Wait. I'll get perfect, and then I'll be ready to get out there and do what I'm supposed to do."

It's a trap. Again, our brilliant egos are taking us on a trip to losing.

Conclusion: Living Authentically

Several years ago, I was interviewing metaphysical teacher Bharat Kalra for *Conscious Community* magazine. He was working with me energetically, and despite all of my efforts, he said that my chakra (or energy) system was a mess. He suggested that I attend a ten-day, silent *vipassana* retreat. (Vipassana is a Buddhist form of mindfulness meditation.) Within a couple of months, I was signed up for a ten-day retreat at the Dhamma Pakasa Illinois Vipassana Meditation Center in Pecatonica, Illinois. The program required us to be in silence for ten days. When we asked why, they explained that during the intensive, we were to practice Buddha's Eightfold Noble Path, one aspect of which is honesty. They reminded us how much we exaggerate, stretch the truth, and are dishonest. The easiest way to avoid dishonesty and inauthenticity is to be in silence. I had to laugh at the truth of this statement. Often as soon as we open our mouths, we risk exaggeration and dishonesty.

As I sat in silence for twelve hours each day for ten days, I was given plenty of opportunities to see the nonstop activity of my mind. I would watch as they did their clutter dance within my brain. As I did, I was able to witness them come and go, like clouds that passed over the light of my radiant heart.

The retreat offered other challenges too. While we were given breaks and meals, for about one hour each day it was suggested that we try not to move while meditating. At the time I was at the height of menopause. I would break out in sweats an average of ten to fifteen times each hour. If you can imagine, trying to sit in stillness and silence while a bead of sweat was taking a slow and steady stroll down my nose was almost unbearable!

Attending this retreat was one of the most difficult and extraordinary experiences I have ever had. It was truly transformative. There were moments where I wanted to jump up from my meditation and race out of there. Sitting with the cluttered craziness of the monkey mind is both eye-opening and transformative. Doing so raised my commitment to experiencing the witness-self more and blasted away any trepidations I had around meditation. After spending twelve hours daily in meditation for ten days straight, doing thirty minutes to an hour each day is now a piece of cake!

Step  3

Step Out of Victimhood:
Owning Our Issues

One of the most challenging opportunities I've had to work with is owning the many ways in which I have considered myself as a victim in my life. It's so easy to blame others for your misery! I have spent many decades doing so, only to find that the more I played the role of victim, the more such situations arose.

The third step in decluttering your brain is to let go of seeing yourself as a victim of external forces, and to own the part you play in the messes in your life. It takes great courage and perseverance to step out of blame and into ownership of your issues.

This can be a tricky topic, because taking responsibility is not about making the wrongful acts of others acceptable, nor is it about blaming yourself for all of the issues that have arisen in your life. In fact, doing so is a ploy for the ego to further confuse and ensnarl you in its web of attack and self-destruction.

The famous Twelve-Step Serenity Prayer offers sound guidance on this topic: *God, grant me the serenity*

to accept the things I cannot change, the courage to change
the things I can, and the wisdom to know the difference.

While I will get into specific examples shortly, it
is important to be clear about issues that arise, taking
responsibility *only* for the part you play in the dynamic.
You can often make yourself either overresponsible or
underresponsible. It is important to have the discern-
ment and clarity to know the difference.

Before you read any further, take a moment to
go through this Victim-Vice Profile. Doing so will
provide you with a greater sense how much you see
yourself as a victim in your life. Once you have clarity on this, you can seek to shift your beliefs from
victim to victor. Doing so will have a profound effect
on your life. You will see a sense of heaviness lift, as
doors open to opportunities that you never dreamt
possible.

Victim-Vice Profile

The more you complain about your life, the more
likely you are to see yourself as a victim in it. As you
commit to raising your consciousness, you will go
through several stages. First, you will want to hold on
to the anger and blame with others, then you will see
how it does not serve you, and finally you will work
towards seeing how you orchestrate the blocks in your
life, consciously or unconsciously.

For each of the questions below, try to be as honest as you can with yourself. Go to your heart and ask
your deepest self for the truth. Then choose the num-

ber that most closely aligns to your situation (1 being "not at all" and 10 being "a great deal").

1. Do you consider yourself a victim of people or circumstances over which you have no control?

1 — 2 — 3 — 4 — 5 — 6 — 7 — 8 — 9 — 10

2. Do you struggle with saying no to others?

1 — 2 — 3 — 4 — 5 — 6 — 7 — 8 — 9 — 10

3. Are you often manipulated and abused by others?

1 — 2 — 3 — 4 — 5 — 6 — 7 — 8 — 9 — 10

4. Do you get super angry at bad drivers?

1 — 2 — 3 — 4 — 5 — 6 — 7 — 8 — 9 — 10

5. Have you experienced many situations in which you disappointingly lost to another?

1 — 2 — 3 — 4 — 5 — 6 — 7 — 8 — 9 — 10

6. Do you believe that you are not appreciated by others?

1 — 2 — 3 — 4 — 5 — 6 — 7 — 8 — 9 — 10

7. Do you have a tough time getting a break in life?

1 — 2 — 3 — 4 — 5 — 6 — 7 — 8 — 9 — 10

8. Do you find others lashing out at you for no apparent reason?

1 — 2 — 3 — 4 — 5 — 6 — 7 — 8 — 9 — 10

9. When you are wronged, do you find it difficult to defend yourself?

1 — 2 — 3 — 4 — 5 — 6 — 7 — 8 — 9 — 10

10. Do you believe that your life is tough and that you haven't gotten many breaks?

1 — 2 — 3 — 4 — 5 — 6 — 7 — 8 — 9 — 10

If you scored between 76 and 100, you struggle, and you often believe you are victim to external circumstances that are beyond your control. You may wrestle with a sense of anger, resentment, or depression. It may be pent-up, and you may find yourself repressing it, or you may be outwardly explosive and bitter at times. The first thing to do is to be gentle with yourself, and know that if you knew better, you would act differently. Self-responsibility can be a very tough pill to swallow, so be patient with yourself, and know that you are heading in the right direction.

If you scored between 51 and 75, you have done some honest and difficult work around your feelings of victimhood, and there are more insights to be gained. The next time you lash out at someone, whether you do so in your mind, or you verbally attack another, make a choice to watch and learn. Simply witness the attacker with compassion and curiosity. In time, you may find the impetus to apologize for your outburst. If not, life will keep providing you with opportunities to look within.

If you scored between 26 and 50, you have done considerable work around decluttering the victimhood mentality from your brain. Congratulate yourself on difficult work well done, and know that you will continue receiving opportunities that call for self-responsibility and ownership for the part you play in the victim dramas of your life. Learning to apologize, then letting go of any remorse or self-judgment is an indication that you have come far on your journey from victim to victor.

If you scored between 10 and 25, you have already done a great deal of work towards experiencing yourself more as a victor than a victim. Continue to note the times that you feel angry and resentful with yourself or others. Witness the resentment rise, and if you can, compassionately watch it do its dance of anger. You clearly are on the path, and the more you commit to looking at your victimhood, the more life will provide you with opportunities to move through it.

Before proceeding, take a moment to review your profile. Do you see yourself as more of a victim than you anticipated, or less? Do you find that you are able to take responsibility for your part in volatile issues, or do you find yourself feeling stuck and powerless? Write about anything that you have discovered about yourself, and have faith that you are moving in the right direction.

Getting Angry at Yourself for Getting Angry

What is the first thing you feel when you believe you are a victim? Most of us feel anger. Anger is perhaps the top emotion that I beat myself up for feeling. It is so potent and powerful that it scares people. Anger can kill. Its might is great, and its passion is palpable. For this reason, I believe, our society is really repressive about expressing it. Yet if it is not expressed and dealt with in a productive and healthy way, it can become incredibly toxic.

Road Rage as a Wake-up Call

I was in my early twenties the first time I noted extreme anger well up in me in a potentially danger-ous way. I had a terrific job at IBM, wonderful friends, great health and a close-knit family. My life appeared to be rosy.

One day I was driving from the office and got into an aggressive exchange with the driver of a Mercedes. Without going into detail, it got ugly. So much so that he drove his car in front of mine, parked it sideways across my front fender, and blocked my way. As he got out of his car and approached my side window, I was terrified. This guy was dangerous. Although I man-aged to reverse and drive myself out of the roadblock, the experience really shook me—so much so that the next day I visited my doctor and told him that I wanted to seek emotional counseling. He was shocked and said, "You? But you are one of the most together individuals I've ever met." Nevertheless, things aren't always as they appear, and I knew that incident was a major cry for help that needed immediate attention.

Since then, I have struggled with road rage for many years. I was stuck in a very reactive pattern until I was able to dig deep and see the underlying beliefs and feelings underneath the anger. To find the underlying truth, for many years I had to sit with the overreactive rage and witness the seething self. Finally, after a great deal of soul searching, I realized that the root of the reactivity was fear—ultimately, my fear of death. I realized that, when driving, I had no control over others, that at any moment they could become inattentive for a split second, and my life could end. Once I realized this and eased up on my self-criticism, I found that the fear dissipated. Whenever I find it returning, especially during heavy rain or snowstorms, I note the fear, and then I say a prayer, asking for safety and protection from the Universe. I find this really helps.

Offering Anger as a Gift

What about looking at anger in a different way? Could you see anger as your prayer, an offering to your Source?

During my teens, I visited Vancouver and fell in love with the mountains and the ocean. I swore to return one day, and I did.

About ten years later, I moved there without knowing a soul, and I committed to creating a vibrant life for myself there. I was going through a great deal. One day, I was fuming. Every cell of my being was on fire with fear, anger, and rage. I got to the point where I felt I was going to explode if I didn't release the emotions inside me.

As I sat on my living-room floor, I started releasing the anger. I was cursing my Creator, with every swear word imaginable. I was raging at the top of my lungs, while smashing my fists against a pillow as if it were the face of all that felt wrong in my life.

Once I'd expended all of this pent-up energy, I got quiet. Then I heard a voice in my head. Instead of the booming voice of an angry, punishing Creator, a gloriously benevolent voice responded, "You gutsy broad! You offered this anger as a prayer against all of the traditions and the conditioning with which you were raised. That is one of the best prayers you've ever sent me, Theresa. Thank you for your courage, tenacity and authenticity. You go, girl."

This exchange with that divine voice inside was delightful. I will never forget it.

The next time you judge the anger that you are feeling, you might try offering it as your gift to your Creator: "Hey, Divine, here's my prayer. I'm really ticked off with you. Here you go. Have at it," and then sit quietly and note what arises from the offering.

Anger Doesn't Have to Be Dangerous

We judge the emotion of anger harshly because repressed anger becomes dangerous. Furthermore, culture, religion, and upbringing have conditioned us to think that anger is evil. We can also label ourselves as angry and become caught in that label. As a result, we often repress our anger, so that by the time we express it, it has built to the point where it is very powerful and frightening.

To remedy this, we can allow ourselves, first of all, to take away all judgment about the anger, and then give ourselves permission to experience it, feel into it. This doesn't necessarily involve a full-scale raging rant. If we catch the anger early, we can allow ourselves to fully experience it and surrender to the feelings that arise, while tempering their expression. When I allow myself to feel into the anger, often I burst into tears. I feared expressing the anger because I thought that there was so much grief that the tears would never cease.

In most cases, underneath anger is a great deal of pain and sadness. But as always, after we are willing to experience the anger and allow the underlying emotions to speak to us, a gift will appear for us.

When We Are Not Willing to See Our Dark Side

Several years ago, I visited the Dachau concentration camp in Germany. As I walked the terrain, viewing the sleeping quarters and seeing the photos of the showers and the scientific experiments that were forced upon the prisoners, I was overwhelmed with a myriad of emotions. I first felt compassion for the prisoners, and then an additional feeling arose that I never expected. I started to imagine myself as one of those soldiers, killing, wounding, torturing all of those people. I had a sense of soldiers having to follow their leaders—because their own families could be annihilated if they didn't—while knowing the wrongness of what they were doing. I felt their confusion and pain.

Some people have gotten upset with me for saying that I felt for the perpetrators. However, I think there's a danger in saying, "Hitler, his soldiers, terrorists, and murderers are all evil. They are victimizers, and I could never be that way. I could never be so evil."

I believe that there is a real danger in that mindset. I think I have the potential within me to be Hitler and to be a terrorist. The moment you start believing that all evil is outside of yourself and you are not capable of it, it becomes toxic and dangerous. When I look deeper, with a sense of inner integrity, I see the wrongful choices I have made, and I see that I am not exempt from evil. No one is.

Getting in Touch with the Pain

Years ago, while living in Toronto, I was graced to work with an outstanding therapist, Mary Anne Carswell. I was so out of touch with my feelings that she had to start therapy by massaging me to enable repressed emotions to arise.

After years of therapy, when I finally allowed myself to glimpse my pain, anger, and darkness, I was able to start feeling the lightness. A sense of joy, laughter, and exuberance arose. I got in touch with my deepest sense of joy and appreciation. My passion was unleashed.

When I cut off anger and resentment (what I deemed to be stinking thinking), I also cut off the depth of good feelings I had. When we can celebrate all of it—the good, the bad, and the ugly—as the human condition, then honor and embrace it, we can experience the wholeness of being human.

Exercise 8: Expressing Anger

Get comfortable in your chair. Stretch if you need to. Take a deep breath in and a deep breath out, quieting your mind and opening your beautiful heart. Breathe out any heaviness, tension, or anxiety. Take a quick inventory of your body, and note any areas that feel tight or stressed. If you find any such areas, melt into them; surrender and exhale the tension.

Now go into something in your life that's really angered you, something that you still feel is looming. Feel into that anger. Feel into the part of you that feels it's not fair, it's not just. Breathe while allowing yourself to fully feel that anger.

Where is it residing in your body? In your solar plexus, your heart, your gut? Go to that place. Let the anger fully express itself. Feel into it. Deeply breathe into that anger.

Allow yourself to remove any blocks. Allow yourself to fully embrace the anger, breathing into it, feeling it, going deeper and deeper into feeling it.

Now if you can, get an image of that anger. What comes up for you? Is there a symbol, something that the anger would manifest as? If so, contemplate that image.

Note its color and texture. Is it thick, like tar? Is it light? Does it feel like glass, perhaps breaking glass? Now do something with that image, whatever it is. Transform it, shape it, engage with it in some way, knowing that it's a symbol, a message from your higher self.

Now, after engaging with it, see that object melting into the center of the earth, melting into the hot, red, volcanic ash, melting and dissipating. It is falling out of your body, falling deep into the earth and fueling it. It is transforming into molten lava, colorful and expressive. See Mother Earth transforming it into something that is of benefit to the earth.

See it now nurturing the growth of a tree, a plant, a flower, and know that that energy, that anger, is now in the ground. It is healing and transforming the earth.

Take a deep breath in, and open your eyes when you feel ready.

Whether images arise or not, allow yourself to go into the anger, surrendering into the feelings. Note how you feel afterwards. It would be beneficial to journal about these meditations if you feel so inclined.

Healing the Shame of Anger

Many of us have put the systems and institutions in which we were raised on a pedestal. You dare not question the hierarchies of religion, politics, and culture, because you are shamed for that questioning. How do we break this shame cycle, which was ingrained into our minds at a very early age?

I think there are a couple of steps to doing so. The first step I take is to I note the anger and rage I felt at the institutions and the way they made me feel, because I allowed myself to play the role of victim for a time.

Be sure to permit yourself that anger, because you don't want to get into a cycle of holding on to the belief that you are evil if you are angry at the systems and institutions in which you were raised.

When I was working with David Hawkins, he said, "The point at which one becomes an atheist is a really good place to be spiritually."

When I asked why, he responded, "Because you're actually questioning. You're not blindly following a faith that you were raised in. In that questioning, you get a deepening, and whether you ever follow a religion or believe in a God again, that questioning expands who you are."

Trust that you're in a really wonderful place if you are questioning your religion, cultural norms, or other systems in which you were raised. If you're not happy with them, if you are angry with them, allow those feelings to arise.

I allowed myself to get really angry. I wrote a poem, which was really raw and angry. By the end of the poem, I came to the realization it wasn't my Divine that I felt had betrayed me, but the institution that told me that it was my Divine. I realized that my vision was not blurred by those in whom I believed, but by the human institutions that perpetuated fear as a means of keeping me in line.

So give yourself permission to fully embrace your feelings. Do some exercises, allowing yourself to feel unforgiving of the institutions, allowing yourself to feel angry with them, to fully express all of the disappointment and sadness, and to be really upset about the shame that you feel has been created within you.

Once you have completed this process, you might note that the shame you once felt is a gift for you to further explore. When I started asking questions, my faith actually deepened. That's when the magic, the miracles, and the synchronicities began to happen for me.

When you reach that point, I encourage you to start looking for the gifts that arise from this exploration. Gratitude brings huge energetic shifts in our lives. Start being grateful. When I started to thank the Catholic church, for example, I was taken to a place in which my spirituality deepened. Where I once called myself a "recovering Catholic," I now call myself a "recovered Catholic." I can now engage in a church service without being emotionally triggered. I am able to honor the traditions and the sacredness that is at the core of the belief system without being tormented by it. Whatever doesn't work for me, I simply do not follow.

When I came to the place of feeling that I was a recovered Catholic, I found a Catholic church in downtown Chicago—Old St. Pat's. It is a very special place: it honors divorcees, all sexual orientations, and the nontraditional. It works for me. It was no accident that I found it, because in my own mind, I had no intention of totally disowning the Catholic church. After leaving it for a while, I discovered that it was still a part of me. It has probably been so for lifetimes, and there's something about it that warms my spirit.

Because I was still committed to that church and I went through the whole gamut of anger, grief, sadness, and forgiving, it came back to me in a way that feeds me. I go to a church now, and there are parenting and adult-education classes where the speaker is so powerful that it's rare when I'm not crying at the end of the session. Old St. Pat's showed up because I didn't give up on the church.

I encourage you to go through the myriad of emotions and confusion. Do not allow yourself to feel shame. If it arises, note it and choose differently.

You may not come to a place where you can forgive the institution. I'm not saying that you should. I made peace with Catholicism because that was a part of my commitment. It may not work for you. My most potent church is Mother Earth. I find a sense of deeper connection and peace when I am in nature. Spending my childhood summers at our cottage in Canada cultivated that connection.

We all have this connection to the Creative Force that started life on this earth. Have no doubt that if you consciously seek it out and definitively commit to finding it, you will.

Hating That You Hate Yourself

As I explored my sense of victimhood and started to own the part that I played in the dynamic of my life, I got a taste of just how much I really hated myself. It was devastating. For the first several decades of my life, I imagined the darkness inside of me as a deep, black tar that was sitting in the core of my belly. For a great part of my life, I believed that my essence was that horrible tar.

How do you start to confront your own self-hatred? I noticed that I'd been lashing out at the world. I was a walking firecracker, ready to erupt at any moment. I was feeling resentful, angry, victimized, and ready to snap. As a very young child, I had a temper that reached the point to where my sisters feared me.

My life coach Frank Mallinder said, "Theresa, the essence of who you are is incredibly passionate, and your passion is your greatest gift. Don't let anyone squelch that passion or tell you that it's wrong."

With each gift comes an opportunity. That passion got me work as an actress. I loved doing angry roles. Auditioners would applaud the contrast and the extent to which I could transform myself (little did they know that performing anger was not such a stretch).

I labeled myself as an angry person; I'd been labeled as such when I was a child. In fact, I heard that label so much that I actually believed that I wasn't Theresa; I was anger incarnate. I started labeling myself as that, instead of as the beauty and innocence that was my true essence. I remember the voices of my inner critic. Whenever I got angry, they would emotionally threaten me and tell me that my very being was wrong.

Throughout this journey, a part of me knew that I had to change the programming in my brain that was telling me that I was darkness. I have spent many years and thousands of dollars working through the anger and the labels. I still find myself struggling at times, but about ten years ago, I started to realize that I was not that tar pit of my stomach. In time, it started melting away, and I started to see the innocence of who I am.

FOCUSING ON OUR LIGHT

We all make mistakes, but as I said before, we tend to hold on to one criticism instead of ninety-nine compliments. We also hold on to one aspect of ourselves that needs reprogramming, as opposed to the ninety-nine aspects that are pure and full of light and innocent. I think that's how we get into the rut of hating ourselves. First, we hate ourselves, then we realize this and find that we can't seem to snap out of it. We lash out at others, and the inner self-contempt grows. The cycle of hating the hatred expands to the point of becoming unbearable.

When I saw others lash out in anger, resentment, and frustration, I would judge them. I hated them.

Sometimes I'd even engage in angry exchanges with them: "They're explosive. I'm going to be righteous. Let me explode about their explosiveness," and I'd have it out with them.

Then the witness-self would step in and observe me judging that person and closing my heart. I would watch the drama as I became very reactive. My body would tighten up, and my brain would be cluttered with critical and angry thoughts.

Then I would sit with that part of me that engaged with the other person, and I would check in with my feelings. I noted how horrible I felt. My inner dialogue would kick in: "I feel really bad. I feel like that black tar. I perpetuated that cycle of anger. I'm no better than them, and I call myself a spiritual seeker." I'd fall deep into shame, self-contempt, and anger at myself for knowing better but not acting in alignment with that knowledge.

In time, as I witnessed and felt into the experience, I gained compassion for myself. I started to see that beautiful, innocent, divine part of myself, which was feeling very wounded. I'd say, "Theresa, love yourself. That anger is a cry for help. It's saying there's so much sadness under here that I think I'm going to explode, and if I let the tears start, they're not going to stop. So what's the easiest thing to do? To lash out at the world. If I lash out, I'm protected from my own feelings of pain." I started to feel compassion for that part of myself.

A Realization in Flight

You know you've started healing when you start to feel compassion towards others. Several years ago, I was getting on a plane. I saw a woman with two children and a husband; she was furious—screaming and yelling at her mild-mannered husband. The self who had not previously done this work would have been triggered by her display of anger and judged the heck out of her. I might even have ridden her wave of anger with her to the point of engaging in an angry exchange with her. For years, like a magnet, I would attract many angry individuals and experience many explosive situations. This is always a sign that there's healing work to be done.

This time, however, I noted that I was filled with compassion. I saw a woman who was frustrated and hurting, and my first thought was, "I have no idea what's really going on." I didn't take on her energy. I noted it, and I noted that it was hers, and not mine. At the other end of the trip, I saw her getting off the plane, just as angry. I told myself, "I have no idea what kind of day she has had." Whatever the case, it was clear that she was in pain. The last thing she needed was further judgment. No doubt she was already beating herself up inside.

Ultimately, I have learned that the moment we pass judgment on others, we are judging ourselves. We're perpetuating our own hatred of ourselves.

Exercise 9: Transforming Anger

Here's an exercise to help you become less angry and more self-loving. You will need a mirror.

Take your mirror in hand, look into it, and look at your face. It might be very difficult to do. Take some deep breaths in, and deep breaths out. You may be tempted to turn away from the mirror. Don't do it.

Keep that mirror and look into your eyes. You may start to feel judgmental about your face, looking at the lines or the wrinkles or the blemishes. Commit to looking beyond, taking deep breaths and looking into that mirror. Look deep into your eyes. What do you see?

Continue to observe, and if you look deep and long enough, you will see your soul. You are the face of God. You are divine. Allow any feelings to arise as you look deep into your eyes. Don't judge them. Just breathe deeply through this. Allow yourself to fully experience your feelings as you do this exercise. You may laugh or cry. Whatever you feel, simply be present with your feelings.

Now begin to caress your face as you would that of a beautiful young child. Honor the beauty that you are. You are divinity incarnate, and there is no one else like you. Look into those eyes and see the hero that you are in your own life. If your life were to be played out as an epic film, look at what you've gone through and who you are. Look at all of the work that you have done. Look at all the trials and tribulations you have been through, as you look deep into your eyes. What a wonderful, honorable soul. See those experiences that you thought were way beyond transforming, the ones you didn't think you could go through—the losses, the sadness, the isolation, the pain. Look deep in those eyes, and tell yourself, "I am proud of you. What a glorious, courageous soul you are."

Let that in. Really let it in. Feel into your body. Is there any tightness anywhere? If so, surrender. Allow that tightness to leave your body and keep looking into your eyes.

You are the face of God. Know that. Show gratitude for the beautiful soul that you are. If there are any feelings of heaviness or darkness in your body, release them now. Send that energy off to the light of creation, asking that it be transformed. Offer it as your gift.

Now see your body filling with beautiful, white light, starting at the center of your heart and radiating outwards, from your head, your neck, your throat, your arms, your heart, up through your abdomen, down to your hips and legs, to your lower back, and into your ankles and feet. You are emanating white light and radiating it out to the world.

Keep looking into your beautiful eyes, and when you feel ready, honor yourself. Fill yourself with love and appreciation. Know that you are goodness incarnate.

When you feel ready, take a couple of deep breaths, and put down the mirror. Write about your experience. You may want to try this several times until you really feel comfortable looking in the mirror. The transition that comes with this exercise may take time, so be patient with yourself.

Self-hatred robs us of the natural innocence that we're born with. I believe it has created a worldwide epidemic. We look at terrorism and we look at violent attacks, and we're not exempt from them. I believe that the terror we see out in the world is a mirror of what we're feeling about ourselves. If we returned to compassion and understanding, seeing the innocence at the core of who we are—all of us—that kind of violence would no longer exist in the world.

As you commit to looking in that mirror, and you commit to honoring and seeing the innocence that you are, you are not only healing yourself, you are healing the world.

Not Forgiving Yourself for Being Unforgiving

When I was a producer and writer at Nightingale-Conant, I remember that the audiobooks on forgiveness were tough to sell. People struggle with forgiveness. Often our first thought is, "I don't want to forgive others. They wronged me and don't deserve my forgiveness." We need to ask ourselves, *whom* do we really not want to forgive? *Whom* are we not going to let off the hook? If we look deep within, we see that it's ourselves that we need to forgive. While this is often difficult to do, I believe that it is a key to opening the portal to living the life you want.

Forgiveness Heals the Forgiver

Let me start with a story. It was one of the most extraordinary things that has ever happened to me. There was a person from my past towards whom I held a lot of anger. He had been very involved in my upbringing. I felt that he had emotionally abused me a great deal during my childhood.

This person ended up very sick, and the symptoms weren't going away. Having practiced energetic healing modalities such as Reiki, I felt a real push/pull around whether to support his healing or not. I struggled with being authentic, because I was not feeling loving towards him. Then I told myself, "Theresa, come on. He needs it. It's a gift you have. Give it."

I went to visit him and asked if he was open to some energetic healing. He's not very open to alternative medicine, but he agreed to it.

He lay down, and I started doing the energy work on him. At one point, a couple of minutes into the treatment, I literally saw his soul. There was no anger or resentment there; it held no regret or vehemence. Prior to that moment, I had seen him as an angry, bitter soul. In fact, I had forgotten that he even had a soul. When I glimpsed his Higher Self, I saw an extremely content, peaceful, and evolved being, so pure that I started to weep.

"What are you crying about?" he said.

"I felt your soul; it's at such peace, and it's so whole."

"You doubted that?"

"Yeah, I did."

After the session was over, I realized I was the one who had actually gotten the healing. I had an opportunity to see into the depth of somebody's soul. Since then, I've realized that we are all pure, whole souls. When I get upset, when I start to judge others, when they behave in ways that I have a hard time digesting, I remember that under the masks of anger and fear, each of us is a whole, highly evolved soul.

This one experience has totally shifted my perspective. I now realize that as souls, we are all so much bigger than we can see or understand. We have no idea how huge and powerful we are.

This realization helped me to forgive myself for my unwillingness to forgive. I was able to let myself off the hook and say to myself, "You know what, Theresa? Your soul-self knows his soul-self. It was just a matter of getting personalities out of the way."

After the healing session, my friend slept through the night. It was the first time since the illness manifested that he didn't cough, and his fever was down. The healing was another wonderful gift, perhaps secondary to the potent emotional treatment that I received.

Ultimately, I realized that I had forgiven myself for my judgments, so I was able to freely and cleanly do the energy work for him.

I've spent a lot of time beating myself up for being unforgiving. It's that old mantra: "You know better.

You've done all the spiritual work. You've done the emotional work. You've worked with masters. You know how powerful forgiveness is. You know how unforgiveness only hurts you, yet you're still holding on to grudges."

I would encourage you to start taking note of the people against whom you hold grudges. Is it time to let them go?

Forgiveness is an inside job. If we can forgive ourselves for being unforgiving, and forgive ourselves for mistakes we made, then we're able to start forgiving outside of ourselves. I find great solace in the saying, "They did the best that they could at that time. If they knew better, they would have done better."

First and foremost, we must apply this principle to ourselves and understand that if we had known better, we would have done better.

Exercise 10: Freedom through Forgiveness
Here is an exercise to support forgiveness.

Close your eyes, take a deep breath, and melt into your beautiful body. With every inhale, breathe into your heart, seeing your heart opening and expanding. With every exhale, let go of any heavy energy, any distractions, or any thoughts that are taking you out of the present moment. Breathe them out of your body with each exhale.

Calling in your Higher Self, ask for someone to come into your mind's eye—a person that you need to forgive, somebody against whom you are holding a grudge. See that person. See the situation and why you're struggling to forgive him or her.

Please note that his or her behavior does not have to be forgiven. This is not about condoning people's wrongdoings. While their actions may have been wrong, to release yourself from the energetic depletion that unforgiveness brings to you, you may want to forgive him or her as a soul.

Now look at that person. See yourselves as children on the playground. You're five years old, the two of you, your beautiful, little souls at play. He is not feeling loved, and he is not feeling included in the games. He is lashing out and behaving with cruelty. See him as an innocent child that is hurting. Look him in the eyes, take his hands, and tell him, "I forgive you. I understand, and I forgive you."

Now imagine your tiny self looking in the mirror, feeling unlovable, feeling isolated and lonely, feeling that nobody is hearing you—that little self, feeling so alone and so lost. Look at that little self in the mirror. Tell that little self, "I forgive you. You made some mistakes, but you were doing the best you could at that time."

Now see yourself as your current, older self. Reflect on the mistakes you've made in your life, the things that you're having a hard time forgiving. See your relatives, angels, or guides by your side, caressing you, holding you, and leading you to that mirror, telling you that you don't even need to be forgiven. "You did the best you could. We love you, and we're always here for you. Release. Allow yourself to see the wholeness that you are at your core. There's nothing you need to forgive. Lift the weight of unforgiveness from yourself." See every cell in your body being washed clean of unforgiveness.

See any of those feelings that are toxic, feelings that are not working for you, as being cleansed. Imagine that unforgiveness being flushed out of your body, starting with your head and working its way down to your feet—flushing, flushing.

Now you feel extremely light. You are whole, and the unforgiveness has been lifted. The unforgiveness has been transformed into radiant love.

Feel your body unencumbered. Feel it light, free, and at peace. Know that it is so. When you feel ready, open your eyes.

Try this exercise with any forgiveness issues that may arise, especially those for which you struggle to forgive yourself.

The only thing that we need to forgive is the belief that we need to be forgiven. When I've sat quietly with my Divine, and I've realized my misinterpretation, I've heard the benevolent source responding, "I don't need to forgive you. All you need to forgive is the belief that you actually think you need to be forgiven. You are doing your best on this earth, your very best at every moment. No forgiveness necessary, no forgiveness needed."

Not Being Good Enough at Not Being Good Enough

Have you ever struggled with feeling you are good enough just the way you are? I have been working on fully embracing the premise that I am enough just existing on this earth at this time. I do not need to do or become anything else to receive an abundance of blessings in all areas of my life.

This can be a tough "opportunity" to work through. Again there's a trap: "I don't feel I'm good enough. If I could only feel that I'm good enough. OK, so I'm going to do all this work on feeling good enough." Then the ego plays a trick: "I don't feel I'm doing a good enough job of feeling I'm good enough."

That's a way to further beat ourselves up—believing that we are not enough because we are not able to integrate not being enough into our lives and to be OK with that. Now that's big-time brain clutter!

It often starts with your judgment of others: noticing that you believe they are never good enough. As a teen, you may tell yourself that your boyfriends are not good enough. Later it may be your children, spouse, coworkers, or friends that you believe are not behaving well enough. Ultimately you uncover the belief that the world is not enough.

Then one morning you wake up and realize that you are simply projecting your own feelings of unworthiness onto the world. What you see in the world around you is what you believe about yourself. Thus nothing and no one is ever enough, and it's debilitating and draining. You realize that nothing can ever make you feel content. I call this *chronic discontent*. I felt a sense of relief when I found a way to label my emotional stuckness. *Chronic discontent* really said it all. I had that feeling that nothing and no one could fill the hole at the pit of my stomach.

Unfortunately, I believe that most of us suffer from this self-imposed condition. You get to a point where you're saying deep inside, "I don't feel I'm ever enough for anyone else. I don't deserve a husband that treats me right. I don't deserve friends that are loyal and supportive. I don't believe I am deserving. If they're acting out, they're only mirroring what I believe. Or they may not be acting out; I may be projecting all kinds of thoughts and ideas onto them that don't exist in their minds, but certainly exist in mine."

Chronic Discontent Inventory Profile

Before you go on, take a couple of minutes to do an inventory of where you are suffering from chronic discontent: where you believe your life falls short of being enough.

Once you complete this profile, you will have a better understanding about how much discontentment is ruling your life. For each of the questions below, choose the number that most closely aligns with your beliefs or with the situations you experience (1 being "not at all" and 10 being "a great deal").

1. Does the question "I want more—what next?" clutter your brain a great deal of the time?

1 — 2 — 3 — 4 — 5 — 6 — 7 — 8 — 9 — 10

2. Do you return to discontent soon after you have a great experience?

1 — 2 — 3 — 4 — 5 — 6 — 7 — 8 — 9 — 10

3. Do you have a sense that your life experiences are never enough?

1 — 2 — 3 — 4 — 5 — 6 — 7 — 8 — 9 — 10

4. Do you focus a great deal on your hopes for the future?

1 — 2 — 3 — 4 — 5 — 6 — 7 — 8 — 9 — 10

5. Do you find yourself stuck in repeat patterns in your life?

1 — 2 — 3 — 4 — 5 — 6 — 7 — 8 — 9 — 10

6. Do you often wish you were in another's shoes, living their life?

1 — 2 — 3 — 4 — 5 — 6 — 7 — 8 — 9 — 10

7. Do you often find yourself envying the success of others?

1 — 2 — 3 — 4 — 5 — 6 — 7 — 8 — 9 — 10

8. Do you spend a great deal of your day thinking, "I wish I had . . ."?

1 — 2 — 3 — 4 — 5 — 6 — 7 — 8 — 9 — 10

9. When you get test results, do you focus most on your failures?

1 — 2 — 3 — 4 — 5 — 6 — 7 — 8 — 9 — 10

10. Do you feel that the glass is half empty in your life?

1 — 2 — 3 — 4 — 5 — 6 — 7 — 8 — 9 — 10

If you scored between 76 and 100, you are struggling a great deal with chronic discontentment. Know that you are not alone. Being aware that you suffer from this state of mind is your first step towards higher consciousness. You can start by becoming aware of chronic discontentment when you feel it. Allow yourself to feel into it, without self-condemnation or judgment. Have compassion, and focus your energy on the current situations that create a sense of satisfaction and contentment within you. If you find that nothing does, know that gaining the insights and practicing the tools in this book will help you to forge a new path, in which you will start to experience cause-less joy.

If you scored between 51 and 75, you have gained some insights, but you still struggle with chronic discontent. Focus your energy on the steps that you have taken towards greater contentment in your life.

Try not to judge yourself and to spend a couple of moments each day focusing on what you are grateful for in your life. When you become aware of the chronic discontent, allow yourself to feel into it, without self-condemnation or judgment. Allow the discontent to inform you, and trust that listening to it will move you in the direction you need to go.

If you scored between 26 and 50, you are making good strides towards shifting your feelings of chronic discontent. Know that whatever you are doing is setting you in the right direction. Continue to focus on allowing yourself to do what brings you joy, even if only for an hour a week. Give yourself the time and permission to experience contentment, and when you do, relish it and express gratitude for it.

If you scored between 10 and 25, you are well on your way to relieving any discontent in your life. Your ability to celebrate the victories of others and to honor your own successes creates energetic movements towards more of the same in your life. Keep focusing on your victories, along with celebrating who you are. Doing this in combination with expressing gratitude will propel you even further down the road of bliss in your life.

Discontent Does Not Have to Be Chronic

How did you do on your profile? You may find that you are more discontented than you realize. If so, know that there you are making strides in the right direction, even by realizing that you suffer from this brain clutter. Maintain your discipline around your emotional journey, and trust that you are taking the necessary steps to replace the chronic discontent that is cluttering your brain with a greater sense of peace and well-being.

Channeled Wisdom

At a time when I was struggling with living my dreams and following my heart's desires, a wonderful channeler said to me, "You know, Theresa, you're enough just by being here. Just being on this planet is enough. If you were to do nothing but feed yourself, walk, talk, and sleep, that is enough. The Divine is celebrating that you have decided to be on this planet, and if you never do anything at all, you are still enough." What a delightful and powerful premise!

Connecting Soul to Soul

Years ago, when I was an audio producer, I was working with an engineer in the recording studio. While we were working with some very famous authors, he was challenging my choices and giving me a difficult time, and he would do so in front of the authors. It was quite embarrassing.

After finishing one particular session, I asked the engineer what I had done to anger him. He responded that he just didn't like people. I was left in a position to consider how to best work with that response.

Three weeks later, renowned metaphysical author and speaker Marianne Williamson was coming into the studio. A lot of audio companies were able to capture her at live events, but I believe we were going to be the first company to do a studio session with her. I was the creative producer of the project, and it was a great deal of responsibility. I was very nervous. I was terrified that when I was working with her, I was going to have the same kind of tension and confrontation during the recording session.

After meditating on the situation, I came up with a solution. I decided that if I couldn't work with his personality-self, why not try to work with his soul-self? Before bed every night for those three weeks, I'd take a minute or two to have an honest and contrite conversation with his soul. I'd express how concerned I was about working with Marianne. I'd then ask if, soul to soul, we could work it out. I requested that together we make it a joyful, easy, and wonderful experience.

Much to my delight, three weeks later, when Marianne arrived, the engineer's energy had totally shifted. He was attentive, friendly, and warm. The recording went without any glitches. It was one of the most delightful recording experiences I had ever had.

When we have difficult times with challenging people, sometimes our personalities can't resolve conflicts, but at the deepest level, our souls are pure, full, and innocent. If the personality has hit an impasse, we need to go to the soul. You might consider doing this if you're having problems with individuals.

Exercise 11: Healing Soul to Soul

Let's go through an exercise in healing soul to soul. Take a deep breath in, and relax, seeing your heart opening up wide, breathing out any fatigue, any anxiety, any unpleasant feelings.

Check in with your body. Is there any tension anywhere? If so, breathe into the tense area to release it.

Now go to somebody you're struggling with. Find that person. Often it's a family member, coworker, friend—somebody that, no matter how hard you try, rubs you the wrong way. See that person in your mind's eye.

Then imagine your higher Self going to his or her higher Self, soul to soul. See that wise part of yourself going to the wise part of that person and saying, "Hi, soul. We just can't seem to work it out personality to personality, but I know we are two whole, complete souls. Here's my request . . ."

Ask her soul what you need of her and what she needs of you in order to shift the energy between you. See her responding in her wholeness, in her completeness. In this place, there's no resistance. It's all surrender and acceptance, love and honoring.

Tell the individual that you might meet again—maybe in dream time—but you're asking, soul to soul, to work together in harmony and joy. Let her know that you would like to free up the personality struggles you are having. See the two of you chuckling with the knowledge that your souls are whole, contented, and pure.

Our personalities are little puppets of the Self. They aren't the real Self. They are little children that are bickering and fighting in life's schoolyard. You're laughing in your knowledge of that, you honor each other, and you thank each other for the wisdom and the commitment towards growth together.

When you feel complete, take one final breath and open your eyes.

You might need to repeat this exercise several times. I repeated it daily for the three weeks prior to the recording session. You might find resistance in yourself. When I was breaking up with my husband, I thought, "I'm not going there. He's the bad guy." But I had to relent and ask myself, "Is this mind-set serving me? Do I choose to be in love or fear? Do I choose to stay angry and miserable, or do I choose freedom?"

If you need to, you might even go to your own soul and dialogue, personality-self to soul-self, and ask for insights about what is really going on. You may not be ready to confront the other person's soul, but when you are, know that doors will open, and things will shift.

My insight from the experience with the engineer was that where there's a will, there's a way to bypass our human frailties. All you need is the commitment and the intention to heal.

I hope these suggestions have helped you see how you have played victim in your life. I also hope they will support you in letting go of the victim stance.

Doing so will better align your energy with a higher consciousness and an elevated vibration. Don't forget: the higher your vibration is, the higher the people and circumstances you will magnetically draw into your life.

Step 4

Find the Courage to Build Intimate Relationships

Congratulations! You have made it to the halfway point. The fourth step towards decluttering your brain is finding the courage to be vulnerable, and in doing so, building intimate relationships.

While we believe that many of our relationships are intimate, as we commit to being honest with ourselves and raising our consciousness, we may realize that what we thought was intimate is based more in neediness. The more I looked into what I believed my intimate relationships were, the more I realized that most of them were dysfunctional. I was often wearing a mask that I thought others wanted to see. I manipulated them in order to serve my own needs. There was not an equal energetic exchange; it was more of a game I was playing to support my own sense of false security while getting my ego's needs met.

Before you go any further, take a couple of minutes to do this Intimacy or Intimidacy Profile. Once you complete it, you will have a deeper understanding of how much you sabotage your relationship with others by avoiding true intimacy with yourself.

Intimacy or Intimidacy Profile

We often struggle with our humanness and judge ourselves much more harshly than anyone else ever would. Through our self-criticism, our brains become cluttered with feelings of inadequacy. Deep down, we don't believe we deserve to have truly intimate relationships. We are afraid to be completely seen for who we are, so we are reluctant to see and accept others for who they are. We tend to put others on pedestals or to see them as undeserving. Either way, true intimacy does not exist.

Take an inventory of how much you struggle with intimacy and your sense of being good enough. For each of the questions below, choose the number that is most closely aligns with your beliefs or the situations you find yourself experiencing (1 being "not at all" and 10 being "a great deal").

1. I believe I'm a wonderful, thoughtful, and kind companion to my friends.
1 — 2 — 3 — 4 — 5 — 6 — 7 — 8 — 9 — 10

2. I am satisfied with my friends. They treat me with kindness and compassion.
1 — 2 — 3 — 4 — 5 — 6 — 7 — 8 — 9 — 10

3. My relationships with friends and family grow stronger and more supportive.

1 — 2 — 3 — 4 — 5 — 6 — 7 — 8 — 9 — 10

4. With family or friends who have let me down, I have forgiven them and moved forward.

1 — 2 — 3 — 4 — 5 — 6 — 7 — 8 — 9 — 10

5. I am feeling really satisfied in my career. I love what I'm doing, and it loves me.

1 — 2 — 3 — 4 — 5 — 6 — 7 — 8 — 9 — 10

6. I have lots of creative outlets. I take time to nurture them.

1 — 2 — 3 — 4 — 5 — 6 — 7 — 8 — 9 — 10

7. I draw loving people into my life, because I am a very loving person.

1 — 2 — 3 — 4 — 5 — 6 — 7 — 8 — 9 — 10

8. It is easy for me to ask others for help when I am in need.

1 — 2 — 3 — 4 — 5 — 6 — 7 — 8 — 9 — 10

9. I am able to forgive myself for the errors I have made in my life.

1 — 2 — 3 — 4 — 5 — 6 — 7 — 8 — 9 — 10

10. I see others having what I want, and I am excited, knowing that I too can experience the same.

1 — 2 — 3 — 4 — 5 — 6 — 7 — 8 — 9 — 10

If you scored between 76 and 100, for the most part you do feel you are enough in your life, and you likely experience intimacy in relationships. You clearly see your worth and have been working on valuing yourself and creating a life of connection. Continue to fulfill yourself, knowing that meeting your own needs frees space for loving others in an authentic way, from a place of self-respect, self-love, and self-acceptance.

If you scored between 51 and 75, your sense of worthiness is quite strong. You are working towards accepting yourself as you are, and others as they are. You know deep in your heart that you deserve a life of joy and connection. Be sure to say yes to yourself more often, knowing that a yes towards your goals and dreams is a yes towards supporting your loved ones in doing the same.

If you scored between 26 and 50, you're struggling, and you need to honor who you are. Start by seeing yourself as an innocent young child. Forgive yourself for your mistakes or shortcomings, and give yourself permission to thrive. As you forgive yourself, you will find it easier to forgive others for their shortcomings. You will gain patience. Know that you were created just as you were meant to be and you have walked a path of courage on this earth. When you can, look into the mirror and tell yourself that you are enough.

If you scored between 10 and 25, you are struggling with a sense of unworthiness and are likely distancing yourself from others. Give yourself permission to express any feelings that you have repressed in your attempt to be lovable, knowing that you are doing the best that you can. Look into the mirror work of best-selling author Louise Hay and commit to changing your mind about yourself and your right to a better life. Work on loving yourself now, at this moment, as you are. The more you love yourself, the more you will find patience and love towards others.

Profile Debriefing

Did you surprise yourself? Are some of your relationships more superficial than you thought? As a reminder, the depth to which you can relate to others is directly proportional to the depth by which you can relate to yourself. In other words, can you fully love, accept, and embrace yourself without needing anyone else to do so for you? Until you can, you will never experience true, unencumbered intimacy in your life.

Not Relating to Being in Relationship

Have you ever thought, "I should just be on a different planet by myself. I'm just not meant to be here connecting with people. I just don't know how to do it right, and I'm just going to zone out and disappear"? I'm sure we've all felt that at times.

Writer Lydia Davis says, "There seem to be three choices: to give up trying to love anyone, to stop being selfish, or to learn to love a person while continuing to be selfish." Many times we think we should sacrifice ourselves for another. Often we do, and we find ourselves disillusioned and disappointed, projecting onto the other person: "They're doing it wrong. I'm not happy in this relationship. I'm giving my all, and they are not."

Being in relationship provides us with an opportunity to discover ourselves on a deeper level. Many spiritual masters suggest that it is a faster path towards enlightenment than solitude.

How Did *He* Get the Experience I Wanted?

In the 1990s, I was studying psychospiritual counseling with Duane and Catherine O'Kane at Clearmind International (clearmind.com) in Vancouver. I dragged my fiancé to a weekend relationship workshop kicking and screaming. He was less than impressed with me and all my woo-woo spiritual endeavors. The last thing he wanted to do with his weekend visit to beautiful British Columbia was to sit in a workshop.

Prior to the event, I set an intention for myself to experience powerful transformation and insights that would deepen my spiritual and emotional connections.

Partway through the workshop, we did a rebirthing session, and in that session, my fiancé went into an altered state of consciousness. Meanwhile, I had my rebirthing experience, but it was nowhere near as soul-transforming as his. He was in that state for several hours, and when he came out of it, he said he felt the Divine and felt himself in this ocean of love. It was so powerful; I couldn't even begin to do it justice by describing it.

I was angry and really frustrated with the Universe. "I asked for the miracle," I thought. "I asked for the insight, and this man didn't even want to go to this workshop." He actually revisited that blissful place several times. I was sitting there in my little corner of the room, thinking to myself, "What gives? I should get this. I'm the one doing all the work."

Then I stopped and thought, "Theresa, the man you love, the man you're going to marry, just had a deep, euphoric, spiritual experience, and that's not a gift to you?" I learned that our desires are always answered—just not always in the way we anticipated.

In retrospect, over twenty years later, I can see how the experience affected not only my wasband, but our entire family. His spiritual experience (which he still talks about) continues to influence the way he engages with me and our daughter. I got a heck of a gift, perhaps even more than if I had experienced it myself. Surrendering into the relationship, however it shows itself, can brings great gifts.

When to Leave a Relationship

One of the most powerful lessons that the Clearmind instructors taught me was to strongly consider and work out any major issues with a partner before leaving the relationship. In fact, their teachings are that you should only leave a relationship when you can completely bless the other individual without any malice or unresolved issues.

I never fully understood the wisdom in this teaching until I was in a mess with my marriage.

We have to be careful with this recommendation: being in relationship doesn't mean staying with somebody when it doesn't work. Nor am I saying that everybody should run out and get divorced, but I can say from own personal experience that I did everything in my power to make my marriage work, and I believe my partner did everything he was capable of to make it work as well.

We got to a point where we were on very separate paths. I was reactive. I was angry. I felt resentful. I'd hear my tone of voice when I spoke to him. I'd see how my anxiety affected my daughter. I hated who I had become in that relationship. That's when I knew that something had to shift.

I had been previously blessed with an opportunity to produce an audio program with metaphysical author and coach Debbie Ford. During our recording session, she gave me a copy of her book, *Spiritual Divorce*. If you are considering ending your marriage, I strongly suggest you read this book beforehand. It is difficult, because it forces you to confront your own role in the broken relationship, and it doesn't allow you to continue blaming your partner for all of the ills in you experience.

I also had an experience with Byron Katie, a speaker and author who teaches a method of self-inquiry known as "the Work," at a workshop in New York City. I believe that she is enlightened (and there are fewer than a handful of spiritual teachers that I can say that about). She teaches tough love. I was committed to seeing the truth of my divorce and to pulling myself out of my victim mind-set. So much so that before attending the workshop, I absolutely knew that I was going to end up on that stage, confronting my issues with her. During the entire weekend, she only chose three or four people out of many hundreds, but I knew I was going to be in the hot seat. I also knew that I would absolutely hate it, but that it was necessary.

I spent two hours with Byron Katie as she drilled me about all of my mistruths and lack of integrity. I was vulnerable and exposed all my dirt. I have never felt so publicly naked in my entire life!

It was powerful. She called me out on a lot of the stuff that I was projecting onto my partner. After I left the stage, none of the other participants said a word to me. Silence like I had never experienced before. I just wanted to get on the next plane out of the Big Apple!

What I ultimately received was integrity. I went home and took steps to get back into full integrity. Then I thought, "What if my partner isn't into integrity?" But I realized that his choices were not important. Now I can look myself in the mirror and know that I acted in an honorable way.

I have no doubt that my Higher Self dragged me to that workshop and put me on that stage. My ego wanted to remain righteous. It wanted to focus on how much he wronged me and avoid looking at how I had wronged him.

When I got to the point in the marriage where I exhausted all efforts through counseling (I think we went through five marriage counselors), I realized I had lost myself in the relationship. I was bitter and angry woman, and at first I tried to change him: "If he could only do XYZ, then I would be happy." Then I tried to change myself: "Maybe I can talk myself out of the anger. Maybe I can force myself to feel unstuck, to feel loving, and to let all my resentment go." At that time, I could not, and I saw no alternative but to end the marriage.

As crazy as it seems, we are now a healthier, more functional couple. Since divorcing, we both coparent our daughter, and we continue to heal the wounds of our past. He now remembers that I hate onions on my pizza, and I rarely interrupt him while he is speaking. Once you have a child together, you know you are still in relationship—for life. When you are hateful, the child suffers, and the two of us did not want her to suffer any more than she already had.

New Hope for Youth

When I was a teenager in the 1970s and 1980s, most of the hit songs on the radio were about finding completion from someone else. One of my favorite movie lines was in the 1996 movie *Jerry Maguire*, when Tom Cruise turned to Renee Zellweger in a room crowded with women and said, "You complete me." I really hated loving that scene. I knew how dysfunctional that comment was, but coming from Tom, it melted my insides.

The truth is that we each need to complete ourselves. Only then will we build relationships that are not supporting our brokenness. A better narrative on relationship is in one of my favorite Kahlil Gibran poems, "On Marriage": "Let there be spaces in your togetherness and let the winds of the heavens dance between you. Love one another but make not a bond of love: Let it rather be a moving sea between the shores of your souls."

Fast-forward into the twenty-first century, and the lyrics of many of today's songs are much more evolved than those of a few decades ago. Many focus on self-empowerment and self-acceptance. Few lament the angst of unrequited or lost love.

Those songs are teaching us that we have to relate first and foremost to ourselves. If, in relationship, we start sacrificing who we are, we need to find a way back to ourselves. To do so, we need to focus on our needs and on how to respond to them, and not expect our partner to do it for us. If we can't support ourselves, how can we expect anyone else to do so?

Exercise 12: Creating Peaceful Relationships

Let me take you through an exercise to assist you in relating to others in a more peaceful way.

Close your eyes. Relax, taking some deep breaths in, and, on your outbreaths, release any anxieties or tensions, witnessing thoughts as they travel through your mind. See those thoughts as clouds and watch them come and go.

Know that you have a right to your feelings. Honor them, and do not judge them.

Now see someone in your life who really irritates you. This can be your partner, a coworker, a family member, an ex-spouse, a religious leader, or a politician. See this person in your mind's eye. Now ask your Higher Self what really bothers you about this person.

Once you've pinpointed that behavior, make a conscious commitment to open your heart and your mind to see what is under the irritation. Perhaps if you glimpsed that behavior in yourself, you would find it so objectionable that you act in the extreme opposite way, avoiding that aspect of yourself at all costs. Or perhaps there's an inkling of that behavior in yourself that you don't want to look at, that you have totally denied and rejected: "I'm not going there. That's not me. There is no way that I would ever behave that way."

Again, breathe deeply into that feeling of what really irritates you. Allow that feeling to move around inside your mind. Make a note of where it sits inside your body. Do you feel tension in your heart area, or your solar plexus? Breathe into that tight place, and allow yourself to fully feel into the tightness, expressing any feelings that might arise. Then allow yourself to simply express and observe. Can you find an ounce of compassion for that person? Are they feeling a lack or a fear within them that is fueling their behavior? What might be going on inside them?

In feeling compassion, you are not making their behavior OK. You are seeing the soul that sits waiting to be seen behind the personality that is acting out. See if you can feel any compassion. If not, allow yourself to sit with your anger, without judgment or self-condemnation.

Forgive. Forgive them their behavior, forgive them their perspective, but most of all forgive you yours. Don't judge the judge in yourself. Honor and understand that the judge is really a little child who's hurting, who wants to be loved, and who wants to feel that he or she is enough.

Breathe in acceptance, forgiveness, and love, surrounding yourself and the other in a wonderful violet light. See it growing from your heart and expanding outwards to theirs. This is the light of forgiveness, love, and acceptance. It radiates beyond your body into theirs, and beyond their bodies into others who struggle with the same issues. Your loving forgiveness is healing the world, filling it with a beautiful, violet, healing light. And so it is.

Remember: whether you initiate change or not, all of those who are involved in a relationship are on board soulfully. It takes two to do the dance, even though it may appear that one is leading. I believe that often divorce brings out the worst in everyone, and frequently there are no winners. Although I was not able to fully bless my wasband during the rawness of the divorce proceedings, I can now say that I do, and I believe we will be lifelong coparents and friends. Thank you for your part in this, Paul.

Energized or Depleted

Years ago, I had a falling-out with a friend. For a long time, I didn't talk to her, and she didn't talk to me. I felt wronged by her, and she felt wronged by me. There are always two sides to the coin. From their perspective, the other person absolutely did right, and from your perspective, you absolutely did right. There are always different ways of looking at the situation; if you'd walked a mile in their shoes, you might have seen things their way. Sometimes there's no right or wrong. There's a lot of gray.

At a high-school reunion, my sister reconnected me with this friend, and it was delightful to be with her again. At times we've said we should talk about what happened, but we haven't. In retrospect, I don't think I need to; bringing it up again wouldn't necessarily serve us.

Feeling unforgiving towards her had been eating me up inside. I lost a dear friendship. Welcoming her back in my life was a means of loving and forgiving myself.

I am not suggesting that you should allow everyone back into your life. Certain people can be toxic. Especially after the trauma of my divorce, as I continued to focus on rediscovering the woman that I lost, I noted how certain interactions drained me.

On several occasions, people who wanted to know how to go about getting their audiobooks published asked to meet me for lunch. I would find myself sitting with them for three to four hours, providing them with detail upon detail on what they needed to do to become published, and then I'd end up exhausted and paying for my own lunch. Do you see something wrong with this picture? Do you see yourself in it?

While I wanted to help people, I was not being authentic to myself. I started to realize that the information I shared had value, and so did my time. I have finally reached the point where I respond by informing others that I have a consulting fee for my services.

Devaluing another doesn't serve either party. If there is not an equal energetic exchange, then one will be imbalanced karmically (or if you don't believe in karma, you could see it as an energetic imbalance). That imbalance ultimately has to come into balance. Once I realized this, I no longer felt as uncomfortable asking for financial compensation for my time and expertise. I was able to step away from seeing myself as a victim, and the anger I felt about feeling misused vanished.

Watch for Energy Vampires

Another thing I've been doing recently: I'll witness and watch. I strongly encourage you do the same. After I spend time with someone, I check in with my body. Am I feeling drained? Is my energy heightened after meeting with this person, or do I feel depleted? If the energy is drained, I ask myself, "Do I want to spend a lot of time with this person?"

Again, change can be uncomfortable. Out of our loyalty and habits with old friends, we think, "Wait a second. We've known each other thirty years."

But if you're feeling drained every time you speak to a friend, you may choose to see them less often. You can still love them, but perhaps at a distance. As you let the energy vampires leave, you create an energetic vacuum into which new friends can connect with you. You have to trust that other people are going to start coming into your life that are more of a match.

With the right friends, I note that my energy is big and expanded when I see them. Practice checking in with yourself around others. At times you may be surprised about who nourishes and who drains you energetically.

Being Prejudiced about Prejudice

One of the trickiest forms of brain clutter I have experienced in relationships is the prejudice that I discovered within myself. I got to a point where I found myself saying, "Prejudice is not an issue for me. I really feel I've come to a place emotionally and spiritually where I am not prejudiced."

Then I started to awaken to the fact that I was prejudiced against prejudiced people. I would find myself judging them for their judgmentalism. There it was again—that paradox that perpetuates the toxic brain-clutter cycle. I was judging the judgers. I found myself feeling righteous indignation against self-righteous individuals. What a mess!

Years ago, I was in an actors' group in Vancouver. We created a weekly mastermind group to support our acting dreams and our allowing of abundance in our lives. Each week we put money in a pot and gave it to somebody in need.

When it was my turn, I noted my prejudice toward those living on the streets. I noted that some were drinking and smoking. I thought, "I am not going to give my hard-earned money to somebody who smokes and drinks. They're going to smoke and drink the money away."

My witness-self then started to ruminate on this, and said, "Wait a second, Theresa. You're being prejudiced. Whether they buy drugs and alcohol, whether they smoke it away, that's not for you to decide. The drugs and the alcohol and the addiction is their pain. What about your own temptations with sugary sweets? Is your addiction any better than theirs?"

So the first time I went out to share the funds, I decided to give them to a smoker or a drinker. I walked the streets, and I saw several homeless individuals who were smoking and drinking. Then I saw a beautiful man with a Santa Claus face who sang and played the guitar. He seemed so sweet and lovable, and I thought, "I have to give him the money." He opened my heart, and I gave the money to him.

A couple of months later, it was my turn to share our funds again. This time I was determined to give them to someone I saw smoking or drinking. I have to confess that it was really hard to do. I witnessed the prejudice in me thinking, "You don't deserve this. I'm not going to have you waste my money."

My witness-self was very saddened by my prejudice. I realized I hadn't walked in these people's shoes, and I had no idea what they were going through. Would Christ or the Buddha say, "I don't think they deserve my love, my healing, or my miracles"? I don't think so.

Again, it was a matter of looking within. How do I judge myself? How do I treat myself when I'm performing in addictive ways or ways that are less than perfect? Clearly the internal judge that is judging the person living on the streets is a part of the same monkey mind that judges me. Since I realized this, I have made every effort to stop myself from judging.

A Huge Gift from an Unexpected Opponent

A couple of years ago, I completed one of my bucket list goals and saw Eckhart Tolle, the best-selling author of *The Power of Now* and other books, at a conference in Huntington Beach, California. While he was everything I'd hoped he would be, I was surprised to find that Marianne Williamson delivered the message that my soul really needed to hear at that time. I have previously produced two audio programs with her, and while I looked forward to seeing her, my focus was mostly on Eckhart.

One of the focal points of Marianne's message was about the importance of pulling out of our egos to ask the Universe the question, "How may I serve?" and to make that our chief aim. I was getting ready to move into a different career in my life, and I found that message timely, poignant, and provocative.

A couple of days later, while writing my one-woman show, I got a nudge to ask my Divine how I might best serve the world. Being fully aware of how often I get caught up in my ego's wants, needs, and insecurities, I immediately responded to the nudge, and meditated on the question. What I saw was extremely powerful. So much so that I began to tremble as I wrote about it.

I've been struggling with the anger, hatred, fear, and hopelessness that was surrounding our political state in America at that time. In the meditation, I saw a political leader with whom I struggle. He was standing before Jesus, who was staring deep into his eyes and said, "I see you, and I love you." The politician responded by hyperextending his chest, like a proud peacock, ready to list his victories, and defend his "successfulness." However, Christ stopped him, and simply looked deeper into his eyes, and gently repeated, "No. I SEE you, and I LOVE you. I LOVE you." In response to that deep love and acceptance, the politician softened into the content, confident, and joyful little boy that he once was before he became laden with the heavy emotional armor he had accumulated throughout his life. When I came out of the meditation, I was moved to tears. My hardened heart had softened.

Then a thought came to me—a call to action. What if we all started giving our fearful minds a rest and started thinking from our hearts? What if we blasted love bombs instead of hate bombs towards those whose beliefs are antithetical to ours? What if we each opened our hearts a little wider with every criticism, hateful tweet, and anger-driven decision we witness? I realized that if I don't open my heart, fear creeps into my psyche. It weighs me down. Life becomes heavier and heavier and more and more hopeless. I don't want to live that way.

Much of the media perpetuates fear, because fear sells. I believe that our political situation has manifested in response to a fear base that abounds in this country—fear of job loss, of scarcity, of the inherent power in women, of violence and terrorism. Ironically, I found myself caught in the web—responding to fear with fear, reacting to hatred with hatred, and championing ignorance with ignorance. It doesn't work!

Now I'm not suggesting that we become complacent or inactive. However, perhaps while speaking and living our truths, we stop fighting *against* and start celebrating what we are *for*. I haven't had a television for seven years. Since noting my recent internal upheaval about politics and the media, I've committed to listening to the news once each day so that I am aware of what is going on around me, and then turning it off.

Some days I go without media at all. I trust that if I need to know something, my friends or relatives will let me know. I skip over the political blasts on social media and watch videos that raise my energy and make me feel good.

It takes discipline, but if every one of us opened our hearts and sent loving-kindness once each day, for one minute, for one month, first to ourselves, and then to those we judge, there is no doubt that it would raise the energy frequency of the earth. Hearts would soften and hatred would melt away, one individual and one minute at a time.

So when I get angry about a politician or a system that perpetuates fear over love, I see golden light emanating from my heart and filling the other with a radiance that raises their consciousness and lifts them energetically. What a gift I received both from Marianne and from the politician!

Exercise 13: Filling Darkness with Light

My Higher Self constantly reminds me that darkness is merely an absence of light, that under every cloud is radiant sunshine. It's time to take you through an exercise that expands your light and radiates it outwards to others in need of it.

Sit comfortably or lie on your back. Take three deep breaths in, and as you do so, tighten every muscle in your body. As you breathe out, allow those muscles to relax. Then with each inbreath, see the light at the center of your heart growing. With each outbreath, see the light radiating further and further outwards. See the light filling every cell of your body with healing energy. See your body filled with loving, radiant white light.

Now, in your mind's eye, see someone you judge. See yourself standing in front of them. Do not send the light to them, but see it extending out from your heart, further and further. See it filling their heart, and then their entire body. See their mind and body as pure light, and imagine their consciousness rising. Breathe their personality-self into their soul-self, seeing any emotional armor falling away.

See their ego-self melting away, and imagine their child self. See the innocence in that child. See them integrating into one innocent, loving, and awakened being. Now look deeply into their eyes. Look at their soul and acknowledge that they have a soul-self that is connected to goodness and light. Keep breathing love and light, allowing yourself and the other to bask in a higher vibration. Allow yourself to express gratitude for the experience and for the lessons that come with this exchange. When you feel ready, open your eyes.

It Takes Courage to Catch Your Judgments

Make every effort to catch your judgments as they arise. Whenever you start to judge someone or label someone as prejudiced, stop and ask, "Am I being prejudiced against these prejudiced people?" If you are, I encourage you to witness it, to note it, to laugh about it, and to love yourself with it.

Your prejudice increases the chasm between you and the other person. When I get onto my righteous high horse, I disconnect from that person, but I've also disconnected from my Higher Self. I'm disconnected from the Divine or Universal Consciousness.

So I encourage you to acknowledge prejudice, but also be able to laugh about it: "Oops! I caught myself at it again." Then move forward and love yourself and love that prejudiced person. The moment we see no separateness between us is the moment the healing begins.

In a way it's a matter of making friends with our prejudice. The more we see these character traits in ourselves as the enemy, the more dangerous it becomes. It separates us. It creates a world of good and bad, black and white, and leaves no room for the rainbow of colors that permeate our existence.

At times when I have struggled with this, I have often asked myself, "How would Christ feel about this?" or "How would Christ respond to this?" I sense that because he emphatically knew and experienced his divine nature firsthand; he had an enormous sense of acceptance, love, and compassion. So next time you judge yourself or others, ask yourself, "How would Christ or the Buddha"—or whomever you follow—"react to this? How would they respond?"

There is a painting of Christ laughing, and I absolutely love it. So often he is portrayed as a somber man. But if you are connected to your divine Self, you see the joy and laughter in many things.

Christ was a charismatic man and an outstanding storyteller, so much so that his parables have withstood the test of time. An effective storyteller has a sense of humor. I think Christ laughed a lot, so let's laugh at ourselves. Let's laugh and love as Christ does. During those times of self-doubt or deep inner judgment, I imagine Christ giving me a huge hug, and saying, "I love you, Theresa. It's OK, my sweet friend. You made a mistake. Let's love it, laugh about it, and move on."

Regretting Regrets

When my life comes to an end, and all is said and done, I do not want to leave this world with a list of regrets. Although we don't realize how much space they take up, regrets weigh us down and lower our energy. They clutter our brains.

Regretting regrets is another game that our monkey mind plays with us. It's one thing to have regrets, but then I actually regret having those regrets. It's a double whammy: That crazy-making voice in your head shouts, "You shouldn't have that regret. You're a soul that's wise and divine, and you know that your life has turned out the way it was meant to. You don't trust that all is perfect just the way it has turned out."

When "What if" Depletes You

While there have been many potential situations that never came to pass in my life, I can safely say that there has only been one regret that I have questioned. When

I was graduating from university, I got a scholarship to study at the American Academy of Musical and Dramatic Arts in New York City.

I had organized a trip to New York with some people from my university theater department. An alumnus of the school told us that this was scholarship audition weekend. He suggested that we try out. So, over late-night coffee and too many donuts, we scribbled out some monologues and songs on caffeine-stained napkins and went for it. That magical thing happened at the audition where I was totally in the zone. I was fully committed to that present moment, and the audition went really well.

At that time, I had no idea how magnificent AAMDA was. Within the week, I got a call from my sponsor informing me that I was awarded a scholarship to the school.

I was delighted, but I was also at the point where I'd paid for the bulk of my room, board, tuition, and books for the four years I attended university. I was exhausted, and I really wanted to start making money instead of working several jobs to pay more education bills. At the time I had no idea of this school's reputation.

The school was wonderful. They called me several times, encouraging me to come to New York; on top of the scholarship, they also promised me work at the school to help with finances. I declined their offer.

Years later I met a fellow actress in Toronto, who starred in the leading role of *Les Misérables* in Toronto,

London, and New York. I found out she had been accepted to AAMDA the same year as I did, and she didn't even get a scholarship. After learning of this, I thought, "Oh, my God, what if?" because I so loved musical theater.

Today I've gotten to the point of telling myself, "OK, Theresa. Let's work this through. You didn't study in New York. If you had gone there, you wouldn't have had your life in Vancouver. You wouldn't have gotten the producing job. You wouldn't have met your husband and wouldn't have given birth to your beautiful daughter." I love the life I have lead and feel deepest gratitude for all of it. I've tried to avoid taking myself on this journey of "What if?" but I can't say that I have completely healed this aspect of my life.

If you have a regret, if it's still giving you a message, if it's still hanging on, there's something up. Regrets are a message that something needs to be lived out and fully embraced. Passing up the academy is the one regret I have. (Well, there was a boy in grade school, but that's another story and another book!) The best I can do to work through this is to allow myself to sing and dance again . . . and that I am!

Effective Acting Demands Presence

After years of doing stage and television acting, I recently realized that performing truly is a spiritual experience. When you see an outstanding actress living the role as if for the first time, or if you see a musician lost in the world that their music is creating, they are in that timeless zone where they are 100 percent committed to the moment. Truth be told, I find nothing sexier or more inspiring than experiencing a performer who is at one with their craft. It is a religious experience for me.

Someone once said to me, "Acting is lying. You're just faking, playing the part of someone else." I was shocked, but as I contemplated his remark, I understood where he may have gotten that impression. I explained that the powerful kind of acting that touches deep in your soul cannot be done unless the actor is fully in the present moment and vested in the role. Through the world of their creative imaginations, outstanding actors make the predetermined, memorized lines and movements their own. Then they delve deep into their life experience to connect with the character they are playing heart-to-heart. When there is not that connection, the performance is flat, boring, and usually hard to watch.

Freedom in Expressing Your Feelings

One of the greatest gifts I received as a trained actress was permission to express my feelings. More than permission, in fact: actors are encouraged to fully feel into and express their emotions. Many of us are taught to suppress our emotions because it may make others uncomfortable. Yet the more I study the ways to higher consciousness, the more I learn that it is not our emotions, but our resistance to them, that creates pain and anxiety.

While many of us avoid doing so, I have been taught that a major part of raising your consciousness is feeling into emotions as they arise. Move with them, allow them to flow naturally. Then you can get to the place where you are totally present with them, and in that presence is the state of grace.

A Message from the Other Side

I'd like to share a very compassionate and powerful lesson I received about regret. My grandmother was dying of cancer. I was going to move back home, and I made the commitment to live with her until she passed. We learned of the news in the summertime. She was in the hospital, and for years, she wanted an air conditioner installed in her apartment. I often thought, "I really should get Nana an air conditioner," but I never did.

As she lay in her hospital bed, I told her that I would live with her, and that I would buy her that air conditioner. She died a few days later. As silly as this seems, the regret that I had for not buying that air conditioner weighed heavily upon me.

I envisioned my Nana saying, "Oh, great. Now I'm dying of cancer. Now you're going to get me an air conditioner? What about the twenty years before, when you never did?" I was projecting all these unkind, judgmental, recriminating thoughts on her.

A couple of months went by. I was traveling throughout Europe for three months, along with studying Shakespeare at the London Academy of

Music and Dramatic Arts. I rented a small room in London during the training session, and as I lay sleeping one night, my Nana came to me in a dream. The love she sent me in that dream was far beyond anything I'd ever experienced as a human. It was so potent and palpable that I woke up sobbing. She really gave me a gift by letting me know there was no regret, that she was in a kind and loving place, and that there was no need to fret about the air conditioner. The gift I received was a deep, loving compassion that was far beyond the earthly realm. I will never forget it. The regret was lifted, and I felt freed of my self-condemnation.

You may not have that same awesome dream, but you don't have to hold on to regret, self-incrimination, and judgment. They only exist in our minds. Our hearts would never permit them to enter its gates. They are more of the clutter that keeps us from fully experiencing all that we are in a life that is only love.

The Gifts of Regret

Regret can serve us in a positive way as well. It's an instigator for shifting and change: "I regret this. Note to self: I'm not going to make this mistake again. I'm going to move forward."

Nevertheless, we suffer when we bathe in our regrets. The energy that was draining from me psychologically (and I am sure physically) because of my "I woulda, shoulda, coulda" regret over the air conditioner was hurting me. Nana was long gone and in a much better place. Goddess bless you, Nana, for returning and sending me that message and delicious love in that dream.

Bodily Signs of Emotional Conditions

As an actress, I find myself fascinated by people. I like to watch them and study the way they move, and I have a theory. I believe that, for the most part, when people have a tendency to lean back when walking, they are caught the brain clutter of their past. If they lean forward a great deal in their gait, they tend to be obsessed with worries about their future. I know that I move headfirst, leaning forward, and if this stance correlates to my theory, I spend a great deal of time worrying about the future . . . and I do! So much so that I had to enlist the assistance of an occupational therapist, who worked with me on correcting my posture.

The next time you walk by a large mirror or window, make a note of your gait (or ask a friend to give you feedback on how you carry yourself). You might find your new insights helpful in further decluttering your brain.

Regret keeps us from being in the present. When it shows up, you are living in the past. It can impede experiencing and enjoying the present moment, as well as looking forward to the future as it transpires. But again, if regret comes up, it's a message. Listen to the message, and respond to it with an ultimatum: "Regret, I am not going to let you run my life anymore. Let's work together, through you. Thank you for showing up and for the message you are sharing. Let's move forward." The more you can move out of regret, the more you can live in the moment and start creating a different and better future.

Exercise 14: Releasing Regret

Let's do an exercise that will help to energetically shift your feelings around regret.

Get into a comfortable place, keeping your spine erect and close your eyes. Take a deep breath in, filling your heart with healing light. Notice any tension in the body and release it on your outbreath.

Now start asking your body, your mind, and your spirit, "What regrets do I have about my life?" See what comes up. "What regret do I need to work through at this moment?" Take note. If no regrets arise, you may be one of the fortunate few who have none, or they may come up for you later on, in your dreams or meditations.

If a regret arises, ask, "Regret, what do you teach me? What is the message you are bringing to me that I need to hear right now?" Then wait for an answer, and ask, "Regret, is there something I can do in my life to relieve you, something I can do to move forward with your message, an action step I can take?"

If the response is no action, that's OK. Just be with that, allowing, and surrendering into any feelings that arise. Once you feel complete, thank your subconscious, your body, mind, and soul: "Thank you, regret. I appreciate you. I hear your message, and I will act upon it. Thank you for being my messenger and my teacher."

Then take a deep breath in and out. When you feel ready, open your eyes.

When we judge ourselves for regretting, the regrets linger. See any regrets you have as teachers, and try not to judge yourself for feeling them. Surrender to them, allow them to melt into your being, and trust that they are moving you to another, more wonderful place.

Intimacy Trumps Intimidacy

Intimidacy issues prevent you from experiencing intimacy within yourself and with others as well. Whether people are still physically in your life or not, you are still in relationship with them. If they sit in your brain as memories, let them be unencumbered by anger, resentment, and unforgiveness. Doing so declutters and creates space for new relationships that are based in intimacy and support your evolving, soulful self.

Step 5

Ask for Help

The fifth step has been perhaps the most difficult for me. I come from a family that encourages independence. However, as I have been seeking higher consciousness, I have realized that my independence is rooted not in strength, but in fear. I have come to believe that it takes great courage to make oneself vulnerable enough to ask others for help, and while I pride myself in my courage, I realize that I am not as courageous as I thought.

We will focus on three traits that can support us in asking for help: giving ourselves permission to need others, allowing ourselves our imperfections, and releasing toxic guilt from our psyches.

Before you read any further, take some time to do this Vulnerability Profile. It will assist you in uncovering where your strengths are, and where there are opportunities for you to allow yourself to become more vulnerable. In doing so, you will further declutter your mind, attract more abundance, and create greater ease and intimacy in your life.

Vulnerability Profile

It takes great courage to be vulnerable. In fact, keeping your heart open and being daring enough to ask others for help takes great fortitude. Answer the questions below. Doing so will show you how willing you are to expose your heart and allow others to support you. For each of the questions below, take care to pause and ask your deepest self for the truth. Then choose the number that most closely aligns to your situation (1 being "not at all" and 10 being "a great deal").

1. Do you have difficulty asking others for help?
1 — 2 — 3 — 4 — 5 — 6 — 7 — 8 — 9 — 10

2. Do you feel uncomfortable telling others you don't have the answer to something?
1 — 2 — 3 — 4 — 5 — 6 — 7 — 8 — 9 — 10

3. Do others accuse you of being a backseat driver?
1 — 2 — 3 — 4 — 5 — 6 — 7 — 8 — 9 — 10

4. Do you stretch your physical strength (for example, carrying items that are too heavy) to avoid asking others for help?
1 — 2 — 3 — 4 — 5 — 6 — 7 — 8 — 9 — 10

5. Do you have difficulty taking the time to help others when they ask?

1 — 2 — 3 — 4 — 5 — 6 — 7 — 8 — 9 — 10

6. Does your family of origin resent it when you ask for assistance?

1 — 2 — 3 — 4 — 5 — 6 — 7 — 8 — 9 — 10

7. Do your friends avoid helping you out when you are in need?

1 — 2 — 3 — 4 — 5 — 6 — 7 — 8 — 9 — 10

8. Do you overexert or overextend yourself in trying to help others out?

1 — 2 — 3 — 4 — 5 — 6 — 7 — 8 — 9 — 10

9. Do you do most tasks, such as painting, moving, and shopping, alone?

1 — 2 — 3 — 4 — 5 — 6 — 7 — 8 — 9 — 10

10. Do you often avoid reaching out when you really need to talk to someone?

1 — 2 — 3 — 4 — 5 — 6 — 7 — 8 — 9 — 10

If you scored between 76 and 100, you struggle with allowing yourself to trust others and be vulnerable. Know that completing this profile has made you aware of your fear, and now you can start to take action steps towards alleviating it. Your fear may be based in childhood issues that have been cluttering your brain for a long time. If you deeply distrust others, you may keep drawing untrustworthy individuals into your life until you shift your beliefs around deserving support. Your first step is to acknowledge the wonderful way that you support others. Then as you see your contributions, you can allow others the gift of contributing to your life.

If you scored between 51 and 75, you have taken some steps towards trusting others. That being said, you have many more opportunities to ask for help and build trusting relationships. Ask the Universe to assist you in trusting yourself and others more. Ask for more gentle opportunities to support you in helping and being helped. Then be sure to express gratitude for the lessons and the shifts that you experience. As you commit to allowing, you will see more and more evidence of help all around you.

If you scored between 26 and 50, you have a pretty healthy mind-set around vulnerability. While you can still expand your willingness to open your heart and ask others for assistance, for the most part, you are pretty comfortable with doing so. Allow yourself to feel into the vulnerability when you ask others for help. Similarly, feel the ultimate joy you experience when you can make another's life easier. Avoid a tit-for-tat mentality when seeking or offering assistance, and relish in the harmony that exists in the exchange.

If you scored between 10 and 25, give yourself a deserved pat on the back. You are doing a wonderful job at keeping your heart open and asking for help.

Continue on the wonderful path that you have created and allow the Universe to show you greater and greater examples of how you are able to both give and receive. Then express gratitude to your Creator for bringing you and yours such generosity of spirit.

Vulnerability Is Anything but Weak

Many have the backwards sense that being vulnerable can be weak. This is particularly rampant in our patriarchal society. If you discovered that you do allow yourself to be vulnerable, congratulations! You have excelled despite social norms. If not, perhaps you will learn to do so in the pages to come.

I recently asked for financial support with my solo show, *Causeless Joy*. It was accepted into solo theater festivals in New York and Los Angeles, but each had lofty registration fees and travel costs. While I was reluctant to ask for help, I knew that beyond the practicality of needing funding, the Universe had been beckoning me to do so and allow myself to be vulnerable for quite some time. So I started a fundraising drive on GoFundMe. I was amazed at how many kind and generous friends supported my dream with the show. One friend donated $500. I was in tears and found her generosity overwhelming. When I thanked her, her response was humble and kind. I was deeply moved. I felt seen, heard, and understood. I felt very supported. It takes courage to ask for help, but when you don't do so, you deny others the opportunity to express their love and support.

Needing Not to Need Others

Needing not to need others has been a huge lesson for me. I am referring to that voice inside that yells, "I can do it myself. I can take care of myself. I don't need any help from anyone." I found myself not only resisting help from others, but actually "needing" not to need them. I had a sense that needing others meant that I was incapable; even more, I did not want to feel indebted to anyone. I believed that if I asked for help, I would have to energetically give back to that individual or they would resent me. While I yelled, "I can do it myself" to the world, I found myself "doing it all" and then resenting the fact that people weren't rescuing me along the way. It's a vicious cycle, and it's a way to stay disconnected from our Creator and from others. It also builds a great deal of tension in our relationships and within our own minds.

Where Is This Belief Rooted?

Needing to not need others often stems from hurts in our childhood. It is rooted in the belief that as long as I don't need anybody else, I won't be hurt. Others won't let me down, because I won't put myself in a position to be expectant of them or indebted to them. I can isolate and simply take care of myself.

Nonetheless, we all need, and we are most needy when we try to convince ourselves that we don't. I've watched my own judgments. I have seen others acting really needy and thought, "Yecch. Oh, my God. This is so pathetic." Then my witness-self steps in, and I observe the criticisms and judgments that I am making. In turn, this triggers me. Noting this fact, I know that I have work to do in this area of my life.

To clarify further: for spiritual seekers, the critical voice within you is your first clue. If I am vehemently judging something outside myself, then I'm really judging the needy person within me.

A Crash Course in Asking for Help

Let me go back to the story about the car crash, because it arose from this sense of not wanting to need others. I was three months pregnant, and I was heading home to Canada. It was a ten-hour drive when conditions weren't favorable. It was winter, I was on my own, and I thought, "I really should take the train." I went back and forth about it: driving in the winter, with the Michigan snow squalls, was not a safe thing to do. But I would have had to ask my neighbor, "Can you drive me to the train station?" and I was afraid to ask for help. It would have taken ten minutes out of her day to assist me, but I couldn't even ask for that.

As I pulled out of my obstetrician's office, I started to turn right towards home, and I thought to myself, "No. I don't want to ask for help. I'm afraid to ask." I veered my car to the left and headed towards the on-ramp to the highway to Canada. Eight hours later, I got into that huge car crash. Why? Because I was afraid to ask my neighbor for help. If that wasn't a wake-up call, I don't know what is.

The Shock and Delight of Being Helped

Often we put out mixed messages to the Universe: "I'm OK. I don't want to need anybody. I'm good by myself . . . Why is no one helping me? Why is no one supporting me? I'm lonely. I'm alone. This is too much for me to handle."

This became very clear to me when I was at LAX with my dear friend and colleague, Dan Strutzel. We were heading to Santa Barbara to meet with former author, spiritual teacher, and musician Luanne Oakes. The airline attendant outside the check-in area encouraged us to wait in the exterior check-in line.

We waited in the line for quite some time, and when we finally got to the front, the official abruptly stated, "You've missed your flight, and you can't get your bags."

"No, no," I said, "but we were just told by the lady over there . . ."

The official proceeded to yell at me. He became very abusive. God bless Dan, who stood up to the man and said, "Excuse me, sir, but you have no business talking to her that way. You have no business being so rude. We followed instructions by your staff, and now we are being told we've missed our flight."

In that moment, I was overwhelmed with gratitude that Dan was taking care of me, that someone was supporting me and speaking up for me. I understood how much I really wanted and needed to be taken care of, and that that it was OK to want it.

We often see neediness as a character flaw. We need, but we think we shouldn't; we should be strong and independent and self-reliant. While that's all well and good, we are, again, taking an opportunity away from the potential giver. We have denied them the gift of giving. When we defiantly say, "I'm on my own. I don't need to ask for help," we're not allowing those that love us to give. The gift comes in the giving as well as the receiving. At Christmas, don't you find yourself more excited about giving gifts to others than you do about receiving them? I know that I do!

Asking Is a Grace for Both Parties

Recently I was going through a deep personal issue. Though reluctant, I reached out to my friend Rebecca. I explained what I was going through and told her that she was the first person that I wanted to talk to.

After sharing, her voice got very emotional as she said, "Theresa, this was a gift. Thank you for reaching out to me. I am honored that you would trust me with this." I received a dual gift. Not only did I receive the grace of her insight and wisdom on the issue, but also the realization that she did not feel encumbered, but was honored by my reaching out.

I'm learning that needing is part of human life. It's part of our human condition.

Traditional Roles and Stale, Old Teachings

Many men have been taught from a very young age that they should not ask for help. They are conditioned to believe that they should be strong and reliable; they should be the one who takes care of everything. In response, many put on the mask of hard, cold independence. But it's hard, if not impossible, to live up to that standard. Many women, on the other hand, have been taught that they don't have to have all of the answers. While this is not always the case, historically in many cases, it has been. Things are finally starting to change, but in my opinion, not fast enough. The other day I asked four different men for directions. I could tell that none of them knew, but they each proceeded to give me the wrong directions. On the other hand, when I finally asked a woman, she simply responded, "Sorry, honey. I don't know."

I could be judgmental of those men, but most likely, if I were a man raised in our society, I'd do the same. Why? Conditioning. Their conditioning says they should be the ones to provide help. Our social or cultural conditioning insists that we should be strong and independent, especially if we are men. It's actually considered a character flaw to need help.

However, anything that you repress or deny expands or grows. If we keep thinking we shouldn't be needy, we risk becoming needier, and in a dysfunctional way.

Beliefs about Neediness

There are two beliefs that underlie this brain clutter cycle. The first one is the belief that I am not worthy. The second one is fear of being judged by others and of not being supported by them. Both stem from that core belief that *I do not deserve support* from others, or from the Universe, for that matter. In my case, I had a history of individuals in my life who responded to my requests with a roll of the eyes and a begrudging, "OK, I'll help, but you'd better remember this" attitude. When you are around this lack of generosity of spirit long enough, you question your own sense of deserving. Of course, if the outer world is a reflection of our inner world, then perhaps I myself had an air of "I don't want to help, and you owe me" when others approached me for assistance. Either way, we are caught in an endless maze of discomfort.

Our world perpetuates the competitive mind-set, and many get lost in the clutter of scorekeeping. Tit for tat: if I give, you'd better give back. My ex-husband's family were wonderful at avoiding that dynamic. If our car broke down, they'd lend us their car at a moment's notice and take the train to work. It wasn't a matter of, "You'd better remember this. Chalk one up for me. You owe me." It was, "Of course. We're glad to help—you are family." I learned a great deal from their generosity and have always appreciated that they modeled a different paradigm for me.

A Misinterpreted Commandment?

For decades I have struggled with one particular commandment, but I finally think I understand it. It is "Love thy neighbor as thyself." Throughout my childhood, I was taught that humans are by nature selfish;

we should forgo our selfishness and love our neighbors first and foremost. I felt a great deal of shame around that particular commandment. The brain clutter would churn: "I love myself too much. I am so selfish. I should love others more. Then the Divine and others would like me more. I am broken. I am wrong." I've struggled with this commandment through the years, and I've finally come to interpret it differently.

We have to love ourselves first, and *then* love our neighbors. Commanding ourselves to love others before ourselves comes from a place of *should*: "You are too selfish. You need to love your neighbor, and then there may be some love left over for you because you did as you *should*." I believe that this way of thinking is backwards. When you love yourself fully and completely, "loving thy neighbor" becomes second nature; rooted in self-love rather than shame, it becomes a choice that you want to make.

Part of the dilemma we face in this world is the *should*-ing. Our society perpetuates the idea of helping others because it's what you *should* do, not because it's what you want. As women, we often feel we have to always give to others, at our own expense, especially to our children. We have to sacrifice and work our way through life. We need to be needed. I've seen many women fall apart when their children get older and leave the nest. The mother has created a life of busyness around serving her family's needs and neglecting her own. She hasn't cultivated a life for herself outside of her children. I have met many women who lived at home for years and were terrified to get out into the working world again. They were unable to see the wonderful skills and practices they'd developed throughout their years of supporting their family.

I feel blessed, because I got the best of both worlds. As a producer, I was able to work from home. For several years, while my daughter was young, I only had to go into meetings one day a week and go into the studio once every month or two to record the audio programs. It gave me a line of communication and a sense of belonging in the world outside of my daughter. I love her dearly, but she's a part of a bigger world for me. I don't need her to need me. I don't live only for my child, and my life doesn't revolve around her.

I am not suggesting that women or men who choose to remain at home to support their families are lacking in any way. Many see their value and appreciate their contributions. However, when parents feel that they *have to* be the center of their children's world, the children can feel it energetically and be restricted by it with a subtext running through their brains: "I can't dare be more independent. My dad (or mom) needs me." Even if that's never spoken, it's still felt. The child makes herself smaller and less independent because she senses that her mother or father "needs me to need him or her." It is said that children who are enthusiastic about venturing out in the world are that way because their home was a safe place; thus they believe the bigger world to be the same. So if your children live far away or are jet-setters, missing them can be difficult, but give yourself a pat on the back. You did a good job parenting!

The Wake-up Call

When I finally realized the craziness of my fear of asking for help, I started to ask, but I noticed that I wasn't getting any. I said, "Wait a second, Universe. I saw the error of my ways and my fear around needing not to need others, so I've actually started asking, but they're not giving. What is going on here?" I started falling into the victim role. I told myself how much I gave and gave and noted how they were unwilling to give back.

Then I worked with a mentor and did some reflection. I realized that although I was saying that I needed help, the energy I was putting out into the world was that I was OK on my own. I was energetically intimidating, putting out a message that I could do what I needed and do it really well. I left friends and family members thinking, "I can't do it as well as she can, so I'm not going to try."

In my overachieving, I was still playing that mantra, "I don't deserve." It's tricky. The ego was saying, "I'm taking all the right steps, I'm doing all the right things, and you're not responding, Universe." But I wasn't really taking the right steps, because I hadn't worked on the core issue of unworthiness.

There is a saying that life's lessons start with a whisper, but if that whisper is not heard, it turns into a yell. While I knew that I had to do more work around asking for help, I wasn't fully vested in doing so. I was avoiding it, until the Universe started to yell the message at me.

Years after the car crash, I ended up suffering from severe sciatica and lower back pains, so much so that I could not do basic functions. I was traveling a great deal for business at that time, and I wasn't even able to lift my suitcase into the airplane's overhead rack. I was ultimately forced to ask for help—a lot!

It's funny how the Universe coconspires towards our well-being. (As a side note, my lower back pain has since been cured, and I no longer need help lifting my luggage, although I often ask!)

Let this be a warning to you. Don't follow my lead. Ask for help now, so that you won't be forced to do so later on in your life.

Conscious Needing Creates Happy Endings

I had a wonderful teacher and mentor in my life, Mary Miller. When I was going through my divorce, she gave me a $500 hologram to assist me with the emotional issues I was having. She gave it to me at a point in my life where I was thinking, "I'm going to start receiving, Universe. I'm going to allow myself to do that." It was hard, because I also kept thinking, "I have to do something for her. I have to give something. No, I'm just going to appreciate her." So I responded to her generosity with a simple, "Mary, I am so grateful." Appreciating and using her gift was perhaps the greatest gift I could give back to her. Years later, I still use her technology to help shift blocked energy.

Now, as I'm allowing myself to need others, they're starting to respond. The other day I bought a freezer. My ex-husband couldn't get it into his car, and I couldn't get it into mine. We were at the store, trying to take it out of the box, doing everything we could, when a man came by with a pickup truck and said, "I see you're struggling. Why don't I take the freezer over to your home?"

I only lived five minutes away, so I took him up on his gracious offer. When I tried to hand him a gift card for his efforts, he refused it. The only gift I could give was deepest gratitude.

This was one among many such situations recently. They are each signs that I am opening the blockage that I had. I'm starting to receive. I am starting to need and ask for help. Look for the signs in your life. The more you do, the more they will appear.

Exercise 15: Uncovering Your Fear of Asking

Let's do an exercise to get to the root of this issue. Get comfortable in your chair and do some deep breathing; breathing in peace and releasing any tension or fatigue on your outbreaths. Breathe into your beautiful heart, seeing it open wide. Breathe out any anxiety, witnessing your thoughts as they go by.

Now see yourself as a young child. You are three or four years old. You're struggling. You're lonely. You haven't yet developed the words to quite say what you need. You are feeling lost and alone. Your needs aren't being met. A sadness comes over you, a sense that you're alone in the world.

Breathe into that sadness, not resisting, and noting any tension that comes up in your body. If there's tension in a certain area, breathe into it. See that tension melting into the feelings—no resistance, just allowing. Surrender to any feelings that arise and allow them to be expressed as they will.

If you don't find anything at the age of three or four, find a point in your life where you felt need, when you felt you weren't taken care of. It's safe. It's OK to go to that place. Really allow yourself to feel those feelings: the isolation, the sadness, the determination that rooted the feeling, "I'm just not going to need anymore. This hurts too much."

Breathe into that feeling. Go into that place. Now ask the Universe, your angels and guides, or the Source for help. In your own words, let them know that you cannot do this alone, and that you need support. See the Divine in whatever way you experience it. For me, it's like Michelangelo's *Pietà*. I see Mother Mary holding me tenderly, close to her body.

See the Divine wrapping itself around you, looking deep into your eyes, and saying, "I understand. You are enough just by being who you are. It is OK to need. You deserve to be helped. You deserve to be loved."

Feel the warmth, the absolute knowing and understanding of what you are experiencing. Feel the Divine holding you, caressing you. Feel the light of its love, starting in your heart and filling your entire body. Feel that compassion. Feel the heaviness of the burden lift, as a sense of weightlessness fills you. Feel its lightness.

Look into the Divine's eyes as it says, "You will always be taken care of. You will always be protected in love. Your needs will always be met. We love you dearly, and we're here for you always."

Breathe into that message, allowing it to sweep over your body and fill your heart. Trust that you will always be taken care of. Your needs are being met and will continue to be.

With that, take a deep breath in and out, and when you feel ready, open your eyes.

You may find this exercise helpful. I find it very comforting and nurturing. If you received any revelations, be sure to write about them. Doing so solidifies the experience and grounds it deeper in your consciousness.

Let me end with a couple of wonderful quotes from author Jarod Kintz: "The only gift I have to give is the ability to receive. If giving is a gift, and it surely is, then my gift to you is to allow you to give to me." The other quote is, "Don't try to hog loneliness and keep it all to yourself. Share it with a special someone."

Consider this next time you hesitate to ask for help. When your friends, colleagues, or family members reach out to you, do you consider them a burden? Is their request an imposition? If so, you have more work to do on receiving help. Note the delight you feel in helping out, and know that you deny others that same delight when you refuse to ask.

Not Being Perfect at Not Being Perfect

Have you looked at your wardrobe lately? I recently realized that most of the clothes hanging in my closet still had tags on them. I had never worn them. The reason: they are my "skinny me" clothes. I realized that the only time I shopped for clothing was when I started feeling good about my figure. When I did, I would go out and buy new clothes to celebrate feeling better about my body. In fact, I was so encouraged that I would purchase clothing that was just a tad too tight, reminding myself that I was on my way to skinny-dom and that I would soon fit into them. Then I'd never reach the desired weight, and those clothes would sit in my closet, accumulating dust as my anxiety about them grew—eventually only serving as moth meat.

Sound familiar? Perfectionism is a tricky game that the ego plays on us. Years ago, I noted my perfectionism and worked "perfectly" diligently to rid it from my psyche. I soon discovered that I was caught in the trap of focusing on being perfect at not being perfect. In other words, my brain was cluttered with thoughts of "Look . . . I've eased up on that perfectionistic behavior. How good I am at not being a perfectionist? In fact, I'm so good at it that I'd say I was perfect at not being perfect."

Compulsive Perfectionism

I noted my perfectionism from a very early age. As a child, if I got a 99 percent on a test, I had failed. I'd be devastated. My parents never pushed me, and they never made a big deal about things, so it wasn't them. It was me. I remember being self-conscious, for example, when singing. If I was in front of an audience, I'd think, "My lips are quivering. They're all seeing me shake. Oh, my God."

I was so self-conscious that I couldn't look people in the eye. I would walk down the street, and I'd be staring at the ground. My mother once said, "Theresa, if you don't look people in the eye, they don't feel they can trust you." I realized that I didn't want that, so I forced myself to look them in the eye.

Perfectionism has been an integral part of me for so many years that I don't think I've mastered this one. On the other hand, a spiritual seeker is constantly searching, constantly going deep within and trying to modify that which does not serve the highest good. There is an integrity in the fact that you want to be perfect, but some of it is imbalanced and misconstrued.

Instead of fighting perfectionism and trying not to be perfect, what about embracing it? Why not give that perfectionist inside of us a great deal of compassion, love, and acceptance?

What if you see that you are a perfectionist, and love yourself, noting that it is a part of who you are? The perfectionism might melt away, or it may still be very much a part of you, but if you can live with it and honor it, you've come a long way.

An Ode to Imperfect Parenting

In a monologue I wrote about parenting, I described myself as "Theresa Puskar, MLE, PIP," the acronyms behind my name saying it all. MLE: for "many life experiences," or if you're really woo-woo, "many lives experienced." PIP: I had seen myself as having the equivalent of a degree in "perfectly imperfect parenting." These were all self-accredited by the Theresa Puskar University of Self-Imposed Hard Knocks.

In my early twenties, I went in for therapy and self-help, thinking, "I'm going to have to get rid of all my woundedness so that if I have a child, I can be the perfect mother." From my early twenties, I was studying self-help and child psychology, although I did not have my daughter until I was forty.

I was terrified to have her. I'll spare you the details, but suffice it to say that moments before I conceived her, I said a prayer: "God, I am terrified. I don't know if I'm ready for this."

A still but strong voice in my head said, "Theresa, stop trying to control everything." Nine months later, my darling Bernadette was born. I worked really hard to be the perfect parent, but I realized that one is never ready for parenting, nor are we perfect.

As much as I had worked on my woundedness, I would still see myself making mothering mistakes. I remember one day in particular. It was tough. I was juggling career with child, child with husband—everything was up: deadlines had to be met, meals had to be cooked, beds had to be made, and doctor's appointments had to be scheduled. I was so committed to being the perfect parent, and I found that I was far from it.

On this particular day, I had a huge producing deadline to meet. I was overstressed, and I lost my temper with Bernadette more than once. I was yelling, and I was just horrible. The last straw was when I saw her shaking as I raised my voice; her little eyes were looking at me, wide with terror (don't forget—I was a trained actress, so the passion—good or bad—was big!). As I saw the look in her eyes, I fell to my knees and burst into tears. I was so ashamed. In my head, that inner critic was shouting, "Theresa, who do you think you are? You shouldn't have waited until you were forty. You should never have had a child. You're passing your woundedness onto her."

Tears were falling from my eyes and into the corners of my mouth. As I tasted the salt of those tears, Bernadette looked down at me, lovingly and compassionately caressed my wet cheek, and said, "It's OK, beautiful. It's OK."

In that moment, with those tears flooding my eyes, memories came pouring into my mind. Memories of good times spent with Bernadette: finger-painting our bodies top to bottom at the Wisconsin farmhouse; laughing hysterically and tearing at a tiny hole in my pantyhose until I could wrap them around my head;

dancing to "Singing in the Rain" together, umbrellas in hand as we strolled down our long driveway during a joyful rainstorm; and watching in delight as we encouraged creepy crawlers to wander all over our bodies. All these memories and more flooded into my mind.

At that moment, when she mirrored the gesture that I used to comfort her—"It's OK, beautiful. It's OK"—I realized it *was* OK. I understood that I was a good mother and that I hadn't visited all my wounds upon my child. Some of them, yes, definitely—but not all of them. It was a huge and powerful lesson, and a gift to me. I needed to give myself permission to be a perfectly imperfect parent.

If you're a parent or if you've been parented, give yourself a break. Next time you raise your voice with your daughter after she spills mustard on her beautiful white dress, or you take hold of your son's arm because he has just finished repatterning your once pristine living-room rug with his muddy boot prints, stop and take a breath. Honor the person you are and the good things you have done. Remember, you're beautiful.

The Perils of Perfectionism

When we judge ourselves for being imperfect, we often hold back on being fully present and fully aware of who we really are. We are spiritual beings, having a human experience. Fine old wines are revered, and so is an old classic car, but as we grow old and begin to age, we judge ourselves. We judge the "imperfections."

I remember seeing a picture of an old native medicine woman. The lines in her face, the mappings of the life that she wore proudly upon her body were so beautiful! Not in the Hollywood sense of beauty, but in the life-lived sense of deeper, pure beauty. Perhaps it is time we shift what we perceive as perfection. We laugh at Hollywood, with all its fake this and that, yet as we age, we think, "Oh my gosh, look at those laugh lines." (I know I do!)

Perhaps we need to shift the paradigm of what we expect of ourselves. It is often said that *perfect* means *whole,* and *whole* means *fully human*, and that includes mistakes.

To make things even more complicated, when I catch myself making imperfect choices and doing imperfect things, I say to myself, "Good. See? I'm not a perfectionist, because I let myself do that." Therein lies the trap: "You see? I'm not perfect, and I'm OK with it" when, in fact, I am not. That game gets perpetuated over and over again.

Goddess Bless Nike!

I have another story I'd like to share with you on this topic. Prior to moving to Vancouver, while living in Toronto, I'd had a lot of temp jobs to support my endeavors as an actress and director. My commitment to myself once I arrived in Vancouver was to make money only by doing creative endeavors. I made a powerful decree about only doing that which was creative, and I stood firm with it.

In response, situations started to arise. When I arrived at the unemployment office, I noticed a poster that advertised a government-sponsored program for women in business. If accepted into it, I would be financially supported for an entire year and given the necessary training to assist me in succeeding with my own business.

The application criteria was not easy. Applicants had to submit a business proposal and additional spreadsheets and support documents. I discovered this program the day before the deadline, and I thought to myself, "They are asking for a huge amount of material. I can't cover all of these requirements. Besides, I just found out about this. I don't have the time to prepare." However, I went to bed that night and had a dream. While I don't remember the specific details, the message was loud and clear: *Just do it, Theresa. Just do it.*

The next morning, I threw together what I could in the few hours remaining. Although it was not perfect, I submitted my proposal and the supporting material that I had.

I got into the program. I have no idea where that wonderful voice in my dream came from. Was it that benevolent Universal Source speaking to me? Did it come from my subconscious? Goddess only knows. I do know that I was called to move, and I did. The program supported me physically, emotionally, and practically. They even ended up doing some media coverage of me and my business. It was a wonderful gift and a testament to the importance of being true to what you want and taking action on the messages you hear.

Had I let the perfectionist part of me win over the voice in that dream, I wouldn't have taken the time to assemble and submit the admission package out of fear that it wouldn't be perfect. I would have found myself in another brain clutter trap. I am so grateful for the voice in that dream, whatever its source.

How Does Perfectionism Hold You Back?

How many times do you hold yourself back from doing something in your life because you're thinking, "It's not perfect yet. It's not where I want it to be"? Commit yourself to sharing what you have with the world, and trust that the Universe will see you through. If it's meant to be, it will happen, and if it's not meant to be, it won't. There's an element of faith in letting go of perfectionism.

Spiritual teachers say that a lot comes through in our dreams. We do a lot of purging, and a great deal of work that we can't do consciously (or choose not to do) is done with us in our dreams.

You may be wondering how to get messages from your dreams. Again, I believe that a lot of it is intention and trust. There was a period where I could not recall my dreams. Before I went to bed, I set an intention to remember at least something about my dreams. I wanted really powerful messages to come through, and I fully believed that they would.

I have since remembered meetings and discussions with different types of spiritual teachers in my dreams. I remember being at a table with Buddhist monks. I remember another time attending a powwow with a bunch of Native American spiritual figures. Later, a channeler confirmed my experiences when she informed me that I would meet and have discourse with teachers while in the dream state.

So I would encourage you to set this intention just before you go to bed: "I am going to have some lessons around X, Y, and Z in my dreams. I am open to them, and I am grateful for the insights I receive." If the dreams don't come immediately, set the intention again: "I want to remember important things in my dreams. I want to get messages." If you do this unyieldingly, they *will* start to appear. All you need do is trust that you have been heard.

Exercise 16: Releasing Perfectionism

Now let me give you an exercise around perfectionism.

Close your eyes, take a deep breath in, and as you release the breath, see your heart opening wide open, radiating beautiful, white light throughout your body. You are breathing in beauty, joy, life, prana, and breathing out anything that's heavy, anything that's getting in your way. As you breathe, witness the thoughts that are going through your mind. Note them, accept them, and watch them pass by like drifting clouds.

Now go back to your earliest memory of being a child. See yourself at that age. Then just scan. Scan times when you felt you were disobedient. Note the apparent mistakes you made, and the behaviors for which you were punished. See them in your mind's eye, asking Source to guide you and to bring anything into your consciousness that may be of value to you at this time.

Follow through the next year of your life, and anything you've done that you've judged as a mistake. Follow into the year after, noting any imperfections. See them coming to you, remembering them, feeling into your body, checking in to see if there are any blocks or tightness. If so, breathe into that tightness. Relax, and allow.

Then follow into the year after, continuing through your childhood and into your youth. Do an inventory of the times that you weren't perfect in your life. See them, experience them, and note them.

You have a sack. Now gather all of those imperfections up and put them in the sack. Bless each imperfection as you place it in the sack.

Now go into the present, to those imperfections you currently hold, those things you judge as imperfect, about which you may feel some shame or regret. Put them all into that bundle as well. Now take that bundle, send it blessings, gratitude, and love. See yourself going to the place where your Divine rests. Go to Source, Universal Intelligence, Jesus, Buddha, Allah, your angels and guides, Mother-Father God,

Mother Earth—whatever or whoever you believe supports you in your life. Present them with this bundle of imperfections.

Now see the Source picking up that bundle. See it blowing its beautiful divine energy into that bundle and transforming it. What does it turn into? What is the image that comes up? Note the very first image that comes up for you. What do you see?

Divine Source is delighted that you have the courage to offer a prayer bundle of your imperfections. With humility and courage, you handed those imperfections over to be transformed and transmuted. They honor you, they thank you, and you thank them, knowing that you can return at any time with any of these imperfections; they are healing and transformative.

Now see how these imperfections have been transmuted. See golden pellets of glorious divine light shooting down onto the earth. Beautiful, little droplets of gold touching the hearts of humankind, touching Mother Earth and transforming her.

When you feel ready, take a deep breath, and open your eyes. You can repeat this exercise whenever you feel burdened with self-judgment, especially around your imperfections.

At times I have even judged myself for constantly seeking, asking myself if I could not be a simple individual, content with the imperfection of what is. However, I can honestly say that in this seeking, my life has been rich and full. Perhaps it is, in part, the perfectionism and sense of woundedness that is taking me to the place of "What is going on?" and then into "Wow!" The magic, miracles, and synchronicities that have manifested and continue to manifest in response to my constant questioning, contemplating, and experiencing are absolutely amazing. Every time they happen, I giggle with delight. My life is delicious, rich, and massive. I wouldn't have it any other way.

As a final thought, consider the makers of beautiful Persian rugs. They intentionally put an imperfection into every one of their creations, because they believe that only Allah is perfect and has the right to create perfectly. If this is the case, as humans, imperfection is our birthright. While perfection may be flawless, it lacks character. There is a charm, a beauty, and a delight in our imperfection. So know that, trust that, and keep darning the imperfectly perfect Persian rugs that carry your life story.

Step 6

The Say Yes Process

In this step, you will learn about my Say Yes process. This technique has been at the heart of the biggest transformations in my life, and I hope it will serve you in the same way.

Before you go any further, take a few minutes to do this Stress or Yes Profile. It will provide you with a sense of where you are stressed in your life, and where you have an opportunity to alleviate stressors by applying the yes process.

Stress or Yes Profile

The degree to which you experience stress in your life is inversely proportional to the degree to which you say yes and allow the Universe to support you: the more you say yes, the less stress you feel.

Many of us walk around with our hearts only partially open to the abundance of gifts that the creative forces have in store for us. *We* are the blocks! Answer the following questions, and take an inventory of how much you allow stress to clutter your brain and impede your life. For each of the questions below, take care to pause and ask your deepest self for the truth. Then choose the number that most closely aligns to your situation (1 being "not at all" and 10 being "a great deal").

1. Do you find yourself overwhelmed with too much to do and not enough time?

1 — 2 — 3 — 4 — 5 — 6 — 7 — 8 — 9 — 10

2. Do you spend more money than you have, creating debt or financial challenges?

1 — 2 — 3 — 4 — 5 — 6 — 7 — 8 — 9 — 10

3. Do you wish you had more recreation time?

1 — 2 — 3 — 4 — 5 — 6 — 7 — 8 — 9 — 10

4. Do you wish you had a larger network of good, reliable friends in your life?

1 — 2 — 3 — 4 — 5 — 6 — 7 — 8 — 9 — 10

5. Have you lost a loved one, moved, changed your career, or had any other life-changing experience in the past three years?

1 — 2 — 3 — 4 — 5 — 6 — 7 — 8 — 9 — 10

6. Does logic usually win over the part of yourself that likes to dream about possibilities?

1 — 2 — 3 — 4 — 5 — 6 — 7 — 8 — 9 — 10

7. Do you keep yourself busy and find yourself afraid to stop or slow down?

1 — 2 — 3 — 4 — 5 — 6 — 7 — 8 — 9 — 10

8. Do you have addictive tendencies that you act upon more than you would like?

1 — 2 — 3 — 4 — 5 — 6 — 7 — 8 — 9 — 10

9. Do you get anxious if you are alone or have idle time on your hands?

1 — 2 — 3 — 4 — 5 — 6 — 7 — 8 — 9 — 10

10. Do you wish you could retire and live the life you want here and now?

1 — 2 — 3 — 4 — 5 — 6 — 7 — 8 — 9 — 10

If you scored between 76 and 100, you are under a great deal of stress. It is time for you to start allowing the Universe to remove the stress that is cluttering your brain. To start, each morning, before you get out of bed, take a couple of deep breaths and see your heart opening. Then spend at least two minutes setting the intention for a wonderful day. Say yes to yourself as you imagine a day that is filled with "yes" experiences. Starting with a strong intention is a great way to clear your energy and start fresh each day.

If you scored between 51 and 75, you have considerable stress affecting your sense of well-being. Start to take small steps towards decluttering your brain from stressful thoughts, even by focusing on your breath for just one minute each day. Each week, do one new thing to alleviate stress. Commit only to tiny steps, and acknowledge yourself for taking initiative. Also use the exercise suggested above and integrate it into your daily morning routine.

If you scored between 26 and 50, your life is somewhat stressed, but not unmanageable. You have taken steps to achieve life-work balance and can continue to create more space and less clutter in your brain. Continue to say yes to life, with the understanding that the Universe will provide. Be sure to express gratitude to the Universe as you experience each gift that comes your way.

If you scored between 10 and 25, you are doing a terrific job managing the stressors in your life. You have come far. It is important to express gratitude for the goodness that comes your way. Focus your attention on the "haves" in your life, and you will continue to see them grow.

Now that you have greater clarity about the stressors in your life, you can start to work on lessening them. In this chapter, I will share techniques that I have created in order to help me de-stress and live my best life.

Listening to the Listener

As I have mentioned, cultivating the ability to listen builds your confidence in the support you receive from the Universe. You are likely familiar with the many voices that you hear in your head: the skeptical naysayer, the constant critic, the fearful fretter.

There is also, however, a voice that is wise and comfortable, bold and bright. It is not one of the voices of the ego or personality-self that are cluttering your brain. It is the voice of your wisest self. It is your Highest Self. That voice watches and listens to all that goes on in your life. It exists and responds to the present moment. It often appears quickly and impromptu. It is enthusiastic and doubtless. It is the voice of the listener, the part of you that watches and responds (note I did not say "reacts") to your life journey. It does not hold angst about your past or fear towards your future. It is present, it is benevolent, and it is all-knowing.

Dialoguing with Your Body

One aspect of de-stressing is listening to and dialoguing with your body. When I was younger, I was struggling with certain physical challenges. I'd put my hands on the part of the body that was in discomfort and ask, "You're trying to tell me something. What's going on here? What do I need to hear?" Then I would listen to that part of the body.

I've done this with my daughter. When she was a child and had stomachaches, I encouraged her to ask her stomach what it was trying to tell her.

One response may have been, "I have a test tomorrow and I'm afraid. Thank you, stomach." Then I would work with her on releasing some of that heavy fear energy. She would speak with her stomach: "Stomach, it's safe. Everything is going to be OK. You can let your fears go now."

Our bodies are wonderful friends. They're there to support our journey and keep us informed. If something is out of balance, they will let us know. For example, if you get really sick with the flu, your body might be saying, "You haven't stopped, and you are going to burn yourself out. So I'm going to stop you before you go overboard."

Be sure to thank your body and heed the advice it gives you. Like all of life's lessons, its messages often start with a whisper. If you get a slight ache somewhere, you can go to that part of the body and ask, "What's going on?" or you can ignore the ache. When you do the latter, the ache can grow. Then you start taking painkillers to keep from feeling it. Eventually that ache becomes a full-blown issue.

Now I'm not saying that sickness is our fault, but our bodies are a part of our energy system. That's why I've talked about experiencing your anger, sadness, or regret. When we're resisting and holding on to feelings without experiencing them, that energy is still in our bodies. Areas become blocked, and the chi, or energy, doesn't flow as it naturally should. The body is holding it. Our bodies are benevolent, and they'll hold it as long as they can, but if we're going to be healthy, we want to respond to the blockages and release that energy. The body talks to us. It tells us what's going on.

Exercise 17: Listening to Your Body

Let's go through an exercise in listening to our bodies. Close your eyes, take deep breaths in and out, breathing deeply, with calm and serenity. Breathe into your heart; see your heart and mind wide open.

Now ask your body for indications or messages. Starting with your feet, ask them, "How are you doing? Is there anything I need to know?" See if you receive any messages. Then go up to your ankles, asking: "Is there anything I need to know?" Going up to your calves, your knees, your upper legs, thighs, hips: "How are you doing? Are you aligned? Is everything good?"

Ask your genitalia, your lower chakra, "Are you functioning well? Is there anything you need to share with me?" Scan and ask the same questions of your liver, kidneys, pancreas, gallbladder, urinary tract, bowels, stomach, vertebrae, spine, lungs, rib cage, heart, lymph nodes, adrenals, thyroid, vocal cords, shoulders, back, elbows, arms, wrists, fingers, neck, head, scalp, brain, nasal passages, eyes, nose, ears, mouth, teeth, gums, skin, and the body as a whole.

Ask your body and mind to allow you to receive any messages that need to be heard. Then be sure to take note of them and respond to them.

Now you are going to do a second scan, a scan of gratitude. Starting with your toes, say, "Thank you, toes. You're wonderful. Thank you, feet. You've carried this body for so many years. You're awesome. Thank you. Ankles, you are so flexible and strong.

Thank you, ankles. Calves, knees—the pounding I do on you, and you keep holding me. I so love you and appreciate you.

"Thighs, beautiful thighs, you hold me up. Hips, you keep me moving, dancing, walking, and running. Thank you, hips. Genitalia, you're such a beautiful part of me, part of the creative process. I love you. Bowels and bladder, thank you for working so hard for me.

"Stomach, digestive system, I love you. You take all that I give you with openness. Thank you. Thank you, liver and kidney and pancreas. Thank you all for working so conjointly together. Thank you, nasal passages. Thank you for that gift of smell, the wonderful fragrance of roses. Thank you for being able to smell smoke in an emergencies. Thank you, nose.

"Thank you, taste buds. I love wonderful tastes. Thank you for working and taking care of me. Teeth and gums and tongue and mouth, thank you so much for taking care, for ingesting. Ears, thank you for my ability to communicate with others, to hear beautiful music. Thank you, brain, for constantly working, sometimes too hard. I love you dearly. Thank you, body, for being so supportive of me, for honoring me and for taking care of me. I take care of you. I'm so grateful to you."

See your heart as the source of light. See it radiating outward and filling every organ and cell with loving, healing white light. Every organ is cleansed. Every cell is balanced, pure, and freed from anything that does not serve your body. See it all filled with beautiful, white light, glowing, cleansed, and pure. And so it is.

When you feel ready, take a couple of deep breaths and open your eyes.

Just remember, you have all the answers within you. All you need to do is ask and wait for the responses.

Being Present as an Active Listener

Many of us are not effective listeners. Active listening takes perseverance and effort. It's about letting go of the ego's need to be heard. I was lucky in being able to cultivate this skill as an audio producer. In fact, it was an imperative. I sat in the sound booth with the authors I worked with, and as we recorded, if I wasn't present with them while they were speaking, they would feel it. Although I had to be ready to ask the next question, if I focused on what was to come, I would lose my heart-to-heart connection with them. Thus I learned to be present as they spoke and to trust that the perfect questions would arise at the right moment. Practicing presence also allowed me to be open to any new information that the Universe guided us towards sharing. Being present was the most effective way to support the author energetically while remaining open to further guidance from the Source.

Experiment with committing to presence while in conversation with others. Allow your witness-self to note when you are focusing on getting the next word in or on what you are going to say. Then let it go and bring yourself back to listening intently. When you cultivate this skill, you will find that your connection with others becomes deeper and more intimate. Your presence is felt, and your connection is much higher than others are accustomed to. People are drawn to you because when they speak, you are focused on them, and them alone. This is a rare gift to all!

Cultivating the Witness-Self

I've already alluded to the concept of becoming more aware of the choices you make through cultivating your inner witness. The witness-self watches, listens, and learns as you act within the drama of your life. You can cultivate and develop it. Both meditation and committed contemplation assist you in doing so.

To pull out of a constantly reactive mode, it is imperative to start listening and watching the drama in your life as it unfolds. It's really powerful: I can be in a drama with a person, and as it plays out, a part of me is witnessing and watching it, as if it were a movie in which I am both the actor and the audience. As I am going through the drama, the watcher (my conscious Higher Self) is coaching me.

A couple of people have said to me, "I'm singularly focused, Theresa; I can't do that," but you *can* set an intention to cultivate the watcher or witness. With commitment and time, you can develop that skill, and your life will greatly change. You might waiver and question, but a new dimension will be added to your experience that will change your life more dramatically than anything ever has.

Not Changing Your Mind about Changing

Here's a little trap that our minds can create for us: "I tell myself that I want to change in my life, but I don't really want to. So I keep changing my mind about changing because if I keep changing my mind, I don't have to go through the process."

When I was working for Nightingale-Conant, we were always discouraged from writing copy with the word *change* in it. One would think that those who are purchasing products on personal growth would be interested in changing their lives, but the word *change* itself was taboo. We had to use words like *transform*, *transmute*, or *shift*, but never *change*.

Why didn't people want to hear the word *change*? The thought of it frightened them. Studies showed that if you had *change* in your copy or your title, people were uninterested. Perhaps it threatens our existing sense of identity and triggers a fear of the unknown.

Of course, there is a paradox with change. We can get caught in the mind trap that tells us that there is much we have to change about ourselves. We have a mile-high list of our imperfections; it is so large that it would be impossible to address all of them.

So there's a fine balance between changing and honoring who you are. The answer lies in discovering and pursuing what brings you joy. What changes make you fall deeper in love with yourself and your life?

Perhaps others want you to change. They may be feeling uncomfortable about who you are or the way you're behaving. However, you are feeling rather comfortable inside of yourself. Then perhaps you're a teacher for them. Honor your desires and trust your feelings.

We have to be careful not to look at externals for a sense of who we are. If three or four people tell you that you need to change, go inside and ask yourself if it is in fact something you *want* to do.

Exercise 18: Finding Joy in Change

Take a couple of breaths in and out and relax your body and mind. Then close your eyes and ask yourself if there is any aspect of yourself that you want to change. Perhaps you have been struggling with something for a long time, and your friends, family members, or colleagues have said that this is something you really need to change, and it's been eating away at you.

Go to your beautiful, innocent ten-year-old self. Is there joy in making the suggested change? Does the thought of it delight you inside? Does it feel right in your heart of hearts? Does it not? Very simply, if it doesn't feel right, it's not meant to be. Trust in the message you received, and when you feel ready, open your eyes and return to the room.

You can also journey in a different direction. You can seek guidance from your Highest Self and ask, "Is this change for my highest good and the good of all?"

Resistance from Those around Us

Whether you go to that innocent child or that wise, divine Self, you have the answers within you. We are often encumbered by shoulds, by society, and by indecisiveness. But it only takes seconds to go within, open your heart, and ask for what is your highest good.

People often fear change because it rocks the status quo. Also, at times we can be lazy. With change comes movement; with that comes commitment and discipline. Although we know change is for the better, we resist it because it will take effort.

You can also lose relationships with friends and family members because manifesting your dreams can rock the boat. When you change, others have to change in response, and sometimes they are not comfortable with doing so. Ultimately, you can only change yourself; when you do, your worldview is different.

When I observed pushback as I made changes, the first thought that came into my mind was, "What is wrong with me? Why are they not supportive?" A dear friend responded, "You are making the changes that they're not making in their lives; you're holding a mirror up to what they're not doing. They are being triggered, and therefore their lack of support for you is not personal. It's not about you. It's about them and their discontented relationship with themselves." Once I realized this, I found the transitions easier. You may regain their friendship or it may reach another level, but it will never be what it was.

Fear of the unknown can arise, and you may question whether you will find other friends who will support you. You may be concerned that you will not find your tribe of like-minded people. This goes back to that sense of unyielding commitment. You can set an intention: "You know what, Universe? I am ready for new friends to come into my life. I am ready for people who are seeking higher consciousness, who welcome change, evolution, and growth, and I know they're on their way. And so it is."

There is a quote from inspirational author Shannon L. Alder: "Your lack of commitment to being different is what kills you. It is the insanity of doing the same thing every time and expecting different results that wastes your time." If you're going to commit to change, you have to be willing to move, to shift, to behave differently. Therein lies the fear. Go to that place of fear. Talk to that fear. Have a dialogue about the change, and watch that fear melt away.

Forgotten Metamorphosis

Several years ago, when I was participating in the Deepening Process at Oneness University in India, we were told that all 450 of us would eventually awaken. My ego was so huge that I believed that my resistance was larger than the Divine Creator. I thought, "I'll be the only individual in the history of this process who is too wounded to be awakened. I'll leave just as I came."

On the final day of the training, we were taken through a process that was the final initiation to the deeper awakening within us. I went through it, and afterwards, I believed that nothing had shifted within me. An hour later, we had a huge graduation celebration. As we ate the magnificent food and hailed the end of the program, a couple of us started talking about our experiences. Each of the group of eight or nine students shared wonderful stories of their transformation. As I sat there and listened, I thought to myself, "Not me. I didn't experience anything. Nothing has changed."

Then one of the gentlemen, a wonderful doctor from Australia, invited me to share my awakening experience with the group. I started to say that nothing happened, but then an image arose from my subconscious. It was a chrysalis. I was spellbound.

I remembered a moment, an instant during the final process. As we were spiraling through the guided contemplation, for a split second, I saw a chrysalis in my mind's eye. A radiant, colorful butterfly had just eaten its way out of the chrysalis. It sat upon it, wet wings gradually unfolding as it prepared to stretch them and take flight. My ego immediately tried to grab hold of the image and force it to change to a butterfly in full flight, but my soul-self would not allow me to do so. The wings remained wet, and the butterfly not yet ready to take flight.

The message I heard was that I was that butterfly. I had just gone through a major stage of metamorphosis, but I was not yet ready to take flight. No matter how much my ego tried to change the image, it could not. I was out of the chrysalis, and my wings were wet. I needed the patience to allow them to dry. Then and only then would I be ready to take flight.

Never underestimate the small images that pop into your head. They are often important messages you are meant to receive. While they may seem insignificant at the time, they are not. You are always guided. There is a steady and strong wind beneath your wings. Your job is to get out of your own way, say yes to life, and trust that that wind will carry you. There is nothing you need to do. Just keep listening and learning, and life's natural metamorphosis will lead the way.

The Risk of Not Risking

Many times I've seen people reflect back on their lives and say, "Wow, I never did this. I always wanted to, and I never pursued it. I wish I had done more. I wish I had taken more risks in my life."

When we're not willing to take risks, we're trapping ourselves. Our egos are playing tricks on us. Our cluttered brains create lists and lists of reasons why we should not follow the leads that magically arrive in our lives. I have to say that, without question, every time I said yes to the nudges I got to jump into the unknown in my life, the outcome was extraordinary, even when it wasn't necessarily what I wanted. The risks were all stepping-stones to greater things. I was grateful that I took the risk and took the dive off the cliff of possibility.

Again, there's an element of decree in this—making a powerful intention or commitment. When you are unwavering in your commitment, when you set your intention with unyielding conviction, you are unstoppable. The Universe has to respond. It always works that way.

I was a professional actress for about fourteen years, and I really loved it. However, the life of an actor can be a little insane: high highs, and low lows. You get a huge TV gig, and you are on top of the world. You get a theater gig, and you are thrilled, then you get nothing for six months. There is no job security.

In the late 1990s, I was living in Vancouver, and I discovered that I had some uterine fibroids. I looked up the emotional connection to the condition in Christiane Northrup's book *Women's Body, Women's Wisdom*, and she said something to the effect that if you're in an abusive relationship with a partner or a career, the uterus is where that issue can manifest in the body.

I didn't have a partner at that time, but I reflected on my acting career, and I l realized that it was extremely taxing and pretty abusive. It was a very difficult life. Yet I lived and breathed acting. It was my heart and my soul.

So I put out a very strong and specific decree: "You know what, Universe? Here's the deal. I will give up the acting and the directing, but I want something that's healing, something that's spiritual, something that uses all of the creativity I have within my being."

At the time I was also getting some accreditation as a counselor with *A Course in Miracles* psychospiritual training at Clearmind International. I really loved the training.

My fiancé was living in Chicago; I was planning to move there when I married him. Clearmind was invited by Nightingale-Conant to do a weekend workshop in Chicago. The leaders at Clearmind invited me to join them in Chicago and assist with the workshop.

We headed there a week before to promote the workshop. As I was walked the halls, I got a very strong intuitive hit that I was supposed to work there. It was an absolute knowing.

We conducted the workshop, and I had a really wonderful experience. Vic Conant and Gary Chappell, the leadership team at Nightingale, attended, and I respected them and their commitment to their own soul work. I left and went back to Vancouver certain that I was supposed to work there.

I don't know where the boldness came from, but with that sense of absolute knowing, I called the president and said, "I'm going to come work for you." He said that they didn't have any job openings at that time, but I said that I didn't care and that I knew I was meant to work for them. He then said that they had just laid off some staff and that they couldn't pay me. I said that they didn't have to at the start, but I absolutely knew that I was supposed to come and work for them.

I guess with my tenacity, there was no room for *no,* and Vic responded, "Come on down." A couple of months later I moved to Chicago. They were doing an infomercial with Sonia Choquette, and they said, "Show up at the infomercial shoot. We have an idea."

I showed up at shoot, and I met the vice-president, who told me that they wanted me to create a coaching program around Sonia Choquette and her book *The Psychic Pathway.*

I showed up the next day, without any specific training or familiarity with the company and their protocol. From that day forward I went to work. I wrote the ad copy for the coaching program, I managed the psychics, I helped to write the curriculum, and I conducted the sales. I was a one-woman show. While my work was far from perfect, I was doing my best, and I guess my effort was noticed. Within a couple of months, they decided to hire me, and I ended up creating and running a whole coaching department.

I said yes to the nudge about working at that company, and my life was forever changed. I worked there for several years, and eventually became a producer. I never imagined loving anything as much as acting, but I did. Now, years later, I have returned to acting. A couple of years ago I incorporated the psychospiritual insights I gained at Nightingale with my acting skills. I wrote a one-woman show, *Causeless Joy* (formerly *Beauty, Bollywood, and Beyond*), which has been at the top of my bucket list. It is an item I can check off that list with the greatest gratitude and the deepest appreciation.

Overcoming the Sales Hurdle

For quite some time I was a one-person coaching department at Nightingale. I had to do the sales calls myself, and I had huge issues around sales. I didn't like salespeople; in fact, I was one of those people who hung up on them in mid-sentence. I thought they were all schmoozers, and I had a sense of their neediness in wanting to make the sale.

The coaching program ended up being highly successful. My sales numbers went through the roof, and this is why: I dreaded getting on the phone to do the sales, so before every call, I would say a prayer and set an intention to make a strong personal connection with the potential client. I didn't want to think about the commission; I just wanted to connect to them. That was my deepest intention. Because my commitment was pure, and the focus was not on what I could make, but on how I could serve the customer, they felt this energy, and the connection was made.

I also received a wonderful gift from the experience. From the way I wrote the copy, some thought that they would receive a psychic reading from Sonia. In the program, Sonia encouraged us all to play with our intuition, informing us that we all had the gift and should practice using it. So in most of the calls, I gave clients readings. Not sure of the messages, I would always preface the reading with the invitation to take what they could use of my message, but if it didn't serve them, they should trust that and let it go.

Doing the readings was a warm and wonderful way to connect, and it instilled in me a greater sense of my own intuitive abilities. To be clear, I don't believe I have a special talent. We all have it. It's a matter of whether we choose to tap into it or not. Again, without question I listened to that inner voice of knowing that rested resolute inside of me.

I encourage you to explore your gut feelings. One of the best ways to increase your intuition is to focus on it. So whenever you have an intuitive experience, where you get a gut feeling and follow it to your advantage, write it down. Doing so brings your focus even more acutely to it, and whatever you focus on becomes your reality.

Don't Be Afraid to Ask for What You Want

I was director of coaching programs at Nightingale for quite a few years. I wrote curriculums and instruction manuals for its audio programs, so I started sitting in on the recording sessions and watched the producers work with the authors. I made a point of quietly sitting in the recording booth with them and listening as they spoke. I served as their attentive audience, and I noted how much they appreciated it. After all, most authors who are speakers are accustomed to speaking in front of large crowds, so sitting in a small concrete, soundproof audio booth can be daunting.

Months after doing this, I went to the vice president and told him that I wanted to become a producer. He said that the company still needed me to remain as the director of coaching programs.

But I was very committed to becoming a producer. I set a strong and deliberate intention to do so, and magically, about three weeks later, the vice president called me into his office and told me that they wanted me to produce programs for the company. I was both thrilled and terrified, having never done so before. Often, when you say yes to yourself and follow your passion, those two emotions arise simultaneously.

I had to risk asking for what I wanted. Many times, we don't. I was willing to risk the rejection, and I think that is key. We have to be willing to risk the rejection, but if we don't take that risk, we will never know, and we will always wonder, "What if?"

Exercise 19: Shifting to a Life of Yes

Let's do an exercise on shifting to a world of yes in our lives. Take a deep breath and relax into your seat. Close your eyes. Breathe into your heart. See your heart opening, expanding. Watch your mind, witness the thoughts that are going through it. Commit to opening your mind and your heart.

Take note of your body. Are any parts of it tight? Relax. Melt into the chair, and breathe in several deep, wonderful breaths.

Now think about something that you've always wanted to do that takes a bit of a risk. If there's nothing that consciously comes to mind, just sit. Allow your subconscious to let something bubble up, something that you've always wanted to do, but fear doing.

Now imagine taking that risk. See yourself taking the action you need to take. Feel the risk, feel your fear. Don't push the fear away. Allow it to arise and express itself. You are safe.

Now imagine yourself taking that initiative, taking that step. Imagine how it feels to take that risk. Watch yourself as it starts to bubble up. You are thoroughly enjoying yourself, and it is a great success. See, feel, taste and smell it in living color and as if it is happening to you now, in the present. You are feeling joy and ease. You are in your bliss. Your energy frequency is raised just because of your willingness to take that risk.

Feel that in your body. Feel the heightened energy that comes out of having the courage to step into the unknown. Feel the joy. Feel the sense of accomplishment and grace. Really honor your courage. See the outcome, which is growing bigger and bigger. Feel into the goodness that is coming to you. You're giggling. You don't know how it's come, but it's coming in waves and waves of goodness.

See how this step is affecting other people, your children, your family, your friends, as witnesses of your courage and willingness to say yes. See what has manifested in your life that is giving them the courage to follow suit.

Now go to a place where your life has come to an end. As you reflect, you see the risk you've taken, and you're watching everybody in this world whom that risk has touched—family members, friends, customers, and clients. More hearts are filled. More souls are living their dreams because of the risk that you were willing to take.

That risk not only empowered you and made your life glorious, but it added to the lives of many others. Feel it blossom fully within you. Acknowledge your courage. Express gratitude to this benevolent Universe for supporting your dreams. When you feel ready, open your eyes.

The 4:00 a.m. Yes Practice

For many years, I found myself waking up at 4:00 a.m. every day. For a long time, I got very upset. I'd sit in bed and count the hours of sleep I was losing, unable to go back to sleep, fretting over the lost sleep.

Finally, after years and years of anxiety, I started doing the yes process I just took you through. I would wake up and allow myself to say yes until I felt it opening a portal in my heart. Then I would say yes to a wonderful coming day. I would imagine it in all its splendor. I would see, feel, hear, and smell a magical, easy, connected, fruitful, and glorious day ahead.

Because it became such a joyful exercise, I often fell asleep soon after, no longer anxious about awakening. You might try to do the same. Give yourself five minutes before you get out of bed and allow yourself to say yes and see a glorious day ahead in your mind's eye. It's a wonderful way to start your day!

I hope you are inspired to start saying a great deal more yesses in your life. At this point, the word *yes* has become a mantra for me. When I repeat it a couple of times, I feel my heart open and my mind calm. A smile spreads over my face, and sometimes even a giggle.

Then I often play music that further inspires the yes mind-set and heart space. When I do so, even after one song, I feel my energy rise significantly. Sometimes I'll give myself yes breaks instead of 3:00 p.m. chocolate breaks when working. It beats the sugar guilt and lasts a lot longer than the temporary high of the chocolate.

Step 7

Choose an Attitude of Gratitude

Did you know that it is impossible to be in a state of gratitude and depression at the same time? The choice is yours, but I find that the more grateful I am in my life, the more I have to be grateful for. In other words, the Universe responds to our high state of gratitude by bringing us more experiences for which we can express further gratitude.

Before you go any further, take a couple of minutes to do this Gratitude Attitude Profile. I created it to help you gain clarity on just how grateful you are or aren't.

Gratitude Attitude Profile

True gratitude can be difficult to "manufacture" if you don't truly feel it. However, the more you are able to cultivate true gratitude and feel it deeply, the more you will discover people, situations, and experiences for which you can be grateful. For each of the questions below, choose the number that most closely aligns with your situation or state of mind (1 being "not at all" and 10 being "a great deal").

1. When you look back on your life, do you have a deep sense of gratitude?

1 — 2 — 3 — 4 — 5 — 6 — 7 — 8 — 9 — 10

2. Do you feel grateful for the little blessings in your life?

1 — 2 — 3 — 4 — 5 — 6 — 7 — 8 — 9 — 10

3. When reflecting on challenging situations, do you often uncover lessons for which you are grateful?

1 — 2 — 3 — 4 — 5 — 6 — 7 — 8 — 9 — 10

4. Can you sink into a state of gratitude and shift negativity when it arises?

1 — 2 — 3 — 4 — 5 — 6 — 7 — 8 — 9 — 10

5. Are you simply grateful for your existence?

1 — 2 — 3 — 4 — 5 — 6 — 7 — 8 — 9 — 10

6. Do you express gratitude for the food you eat, your home, and your conveniences?

1 — 2 — 3 — 4 — 5 — 6 — 7 — 8 — 9 — 10

7. Do you frequently say thank-you throughout your day?

1 — 2 — 3 — 4 — 5 — 6 — 7 — 8 — 9 — 10

8. Do others frequently express gratitude to you?

1 — 2 — 3 — 4 — 5 — 6 — 7 — 8 — 9 — 10

9. Do you express gratitude for the beauties of nature, the arts, or other phenomena of creation?

1 — 2 — 3 — 4 — 5 — 6 — 7 — 8 — 9 — 10

10. Do you feel gratitude towards your future, along with your past and present?

1 — 2 — 3 — 4 — 5 — 6 — 7 — 8 — 9 — 10

If you scored between 76 and 100, you exude gratitude in your life, and you have much to be grateful for. You have likely discovered that the more grateful you feel, the more miracles come your way. Pay attention to the myriad of synchronicities that occur in your life. Ask for them, expect them to continue, and acknowledge them when they do. Gratitude energizes you and raises your consciousness and your quality of life.

If you scored between 51 and 75, you have a great deal to be grateful for in your life and you are pretty effective at expressing it. To create an even greater gratitude attitude, make a point of finding at least three things to be grateful for each day. Your commitment to live in gratitude turns challenges into opportunities and upsets into matters for introspection.

If you scored between 26 and 50, your gratitude attitude could use some improvement. Allow yourself to consciously look for things to be grateful for throughout your day. It might help to keep a gratitude journal or write a list of at least three things you are grateful for at the end of each day. You may want to write a list of all that you are grateful for in your life. Then read the list at least once a week and add to it when you are inspired to do so.

If you scored between 10 and 25, you are focusing more on what you lack than on what you are grateful for in your life. You might want to start with yourself. What do you most respect about yourself? What choices have you made in your life that you are proud of, but never really appreciated about yourself? Start acknowledging yourself, and then extend your gratitude and appreciation to others. As you do, you will shift from lack consciousness to an attitude of gratitude.

Appreciating What Is

In India, our teacher told us that most of us were lacking in gratitude. I thought I was pretty good at expressing appreciation until I committed to inner integrity and asked to see the truth. Much to my dismay, I started to see just how ungrateful I had been. I would often find myself doing a very quick, "Thanks, Universe" and then returning to my list of "I want more. I want . . . and I want . . ."

Again, we must take care not to shame ourselves for wanting, but it is interesting to note how much we can get lost in the world of what I want, and gloss over what is!

Being Stuck on Feeling Stuck

Many of us catch ourselves feeling stuck, and I think there are two aspects to this subject. There is the position of feeling stuck in your own web of brain clutter, and then there's feeling stuck in other people's stuckness. Very often, without knowing it, we can get pulled into the energy that others are emitting, and it can bring down our own energy drastically.

I love the teachings of channelor Esther Hicks. She channels spirit guides known as Abraham.* They say that contrast is a good thing. If we find ourselves in a certain situation or predicament that does not work for us, it provides contrast. It's informing us of our current state in comparison to where we want to be. According to Abraham's wisdom, we experience more and more contrast until we hit a breaking point, at which time we say, "I don't like this anymore. I'm shifting it." And we do.

From that perspective, nobody is ever stuck. You can't do it wrong, and you will never get it all done. Life is constantly evolving, and we are as well. As soon as one desire manifests in reality, another will appear. There's a continuum, a journey. At the point where we feel stuck, we can make the choice to get unstuck.

---

* The Abraham-Hicks teachings are a major inspiration for the Law of Attraction wave that is sweeping the world, and for thousands of books, films, essays, and lectures that are responsible for the current paradigm shift in consciousness.

Running Away from a Stuck Relationship

Years ago, I was in a relationship that was not emotionally satisfying. The gentleman I was dating was in love with his ex-girlfriend, who was teaching English in Japan. There was a disconnect between us that was very palpable. However, I felt stuck in the relationship, because although I was miserable with the man, I didn't want to be alone.

What did I do? I ran off to Europe. I gave myself distance and space from him and the sticky situation I was in. Do I suggest that you do the same? Only you would know what is best for you.

From the get-go, the trip was extraordinary. When I told my acting agent in Toronto that I was heading to Europe for three months, she encouraged me to research some good acting schools in London, so that I could add them to my résumé. When I arrived, I asked a friend I was staying with in London where I might find a good acting school. She suggested that I check out Regent's University. The next day I headed to Regent's, and upon my arrival, I asked if there were any acting schools that were offering summer programs in the area. I was soon directed to a room down the hall, where several people were packing boxes. When I investigated, they told me that they were on their way to Oxford the next day. They were BADA (the British Academy of Dramatic Arts), and they had joined forces with Yale Graduate School to offer a six-week summer acting intensive program. Exactly what I wanted.

When they showed me the brochure, I saw a list of famous, exceptional actors and directors in it. I wondered if they were actually teaching or were simply listed as associates or board members. Much to my surprise, they were teaching! The director asked if I would like to audition for the program. So in the gardens of Regent's University, I recited two monologues, one Shakespearean and one contemporary. They immediately informed me that I was accepted into the school. I don't believe they made the offer because I was brilliant (although my audition was OK). I believe that they may have had a couple of last-minute cancellations and needed to fill the spots.

When I asked the cost, they informed me that it was something like $6,000. I told them that I had nowhere near that amount. They informed me that they would charge $1,500 for board and tuition for the program. I was elated. The program started the next day, so I was on my way.

The training was extraordinary. I studied with Jeremy Irons, Vanessa Redgrave, Brian Cox, and Rosemary Harris, among others. After the program ended, I headed down to Corfu, Greece, because I had few funds left and Greece was a cheap and magical place to visit.

I ended up meeting a wonderful lady, Greta, in the train station in Rome. I shared some biscuits and water with her, and in return, she invited me to spend a month touring six Greek islands, with room, board, and excursions all completely paid for. (The friend she was going with had gotten homesick, and the costs of the tour could not be refunded). I had an amazing time with Greta, and the entire trip was one amazing experience. When I arrived back in Toronto, I felt ready to move on and left the relationship, no longer feeling stuck.

I don't fully understand why I had such an exceptional experience during that trip. It was absolutely magical. Whatever hand led me in that direction, I moved where my spirit called, and in response, I was freed from that sense of being stuck.

Discomfort with Emotional Expression

Sometimes we see that others are stuck, and we want to help them get unstuck. It often comes from our own discomfort with the stuckness.

I suggest that you experiment with something. The next time someone cries in your presence, whether personally or publicly at a workshop, see if you can simply be present with the tears. Often someone breaks the energy and grabs a box of tissues. This drives me insane. If I want a tissue, I'll reach for one. Most often, the one who grab the tissues will tell themselves that they are just being helpful. But if you look deeper, most often the gesture is rooted in their own discomfort with emotion. I encourage you to sit and witness the emotional release without trying to comfort the person. Simply be present and know that being so is a wonderful way to support and acknowledge the individual.

Stuck on the Stuckness of Others

As I have mentioned, you can also get lost in the stuckness of others, and in doing so, you can lose a great deal of energy. I have found myself ruminating about a person, worrying, "How can I help her get unstuck? What can I do?" In my discomfort with her stuckness, I'd try and find solutions for her. Then I'd get on the phone and become her personal coach: "I have a great idea. Why don't you do this?" She would respond with a half-hearted commitment. I'd give other ideas, constantly trying to find opportunities for her. She wouldn't take action on my suggestions, but would continue to complain about how stuck she was. I would feel frustrated and anxious because I could see the person's potential. I could see how she could get unstuck and move forward, but she chose not to take any action.

If I watch in these situations, do I see her energy rise in any way when I try to help her get unstuck? No. In fact, it probably drops because she is shaming herself for not taking the steps that I suggested.

Ultimately, we both lose energy in this dynamic. I feel defeated; she feels ashamed. It does no one any good. Again, the best way to support our friends and family is to be present with them, and to hold the space for growth if and when they are ready.

Work on getting unstuck from your own stuckness. Give others permission to be stuck. As Abraham says, when they have eventually experienced enough contrast, they will do something about it. Either way, it is not your problem.

Realize that while being stuck may be a challenge, staying stuck is a choice. You need to give them permission and space to take their own spiritual journey. By being too much of a helper, you are depriving them of the lessons and experiences that their souls have committed to. You can do more harm than good by trying to help them get unstuck.

Stuckness can be a catalyst. When you get to the point where you've had enough, you will ask, and the Universe will hear that, so a shift will take place. You may take a lot of time; you may take very little time. Honor where you're at. Don't judge yourself for your stuckness. Don't do the *should*-ing: "I'm evolved. I know how to move forward. I do motivational programs with spiritual masters. Why am I stuck? I really shouldn't be here."

The mantra "You should know better" may rear its ugly head.

Again, see yourself as an innocent, young child. If your child was crying, "Mommy, I can't get out of here. I'm stuck in the mud," would you judge and beat that child? No. You'd either help her out or join her and play in the mud with her.

Honor and accept the stuckness, and then try to move through it, or trust that when you can no longer tolerate it, you will move through it.

Exercise 20: Moving Yourself Forward

The way to get unstuck is to see yourself moving forward. Here's a visualization for this.

Take a deep breath and close your eyes. See any tension in your body, melting away. Take a moment to reflect on all the things you are grateful for in your life. Allow yourself to feel into that gratitude. Thank the Universe for the wonderful relationships you have. Express gratitude for the magical experiences that have filled your life.

Now allow yourself to focus on an area in which you feel stuck, where you don't feel you can move forward. Now see yourself taking a little step, one very small step.

It doesn't have to be big—just a little, tiny step, something that feels good. For example, if you're a mother, you're stuck at home, and you feel you have no time to yourself, perhaps you can see yourself taking five minutes a week to write or to listen to a piece of music that takes you to another place. Visualize doing something that takes you a step closer to a better-feeling place.

Now imagine yourself getting unstuck. What would that look like? If you're stuck in a career you don't enjoy or are in a difficult marriage, imagine being free of that stuckness. Imagine joy. Imagine relating to the other person or to the situation in a way that is liberating.

Imagine yourself feeling free, joyful, and unencumbered. Feel the bliss; feel the joy. If you can't get to the place where you're feeling unstuck, go to a place where you feel just a little bit better.

Take a Bliss Break

Visualizing and expressing gratitude are wonderful exercises that can assist you in feeling less stuck. Another technique is to go to a better-feeling place. Perhaps it's listening to a piece of music. One of my favorite music breaks is the Black Eyed Peas' flash mob of "I Gotta Feeling" on the Oprah Show. If you haven't watched it, you should really go to YouTube and put it on. There are 22,000 people surprising Oprah and dancing in tandem. Whenever I see it, I can't help being filled with joy! When I was going through some rough times, I'd go into the office, close the door, and put that video on. It totally shifted my energy. At times when I felt stuck and hopeless, that video took me to a better place.

If you find yourself stuck and unable to move forward, sing, dance, write, do pottery, read a book—do whatever brings you joy, even if it is only for five minutes a day. Go to that better-feeling place with intention, commitment, and the knowledge that eventually you will get unstuck.

Trying to Control Being out of Control

Control is a big word. Some people say, "Take control of your life," and others say, "You have no control, so give it up."

In fact, trying to force control in your life constricts you energetically. Allowing builds energy and creates emotional space in your psyche. I like to use the analogy of asthma. In the past, I struggled with asthma. When my lungs became congested, I would lower my shoulders, tighten my chest, and constrict the air further.

One day my friend Yvette suggested, "Do the opposite. When you feel your body and lungs tightening up, pull your chest out. Put your shoulders back and create space." I noted that as I did this, I was able to breathe more deeply. I was able to fill the lungs more, and within minutes the congestion started to dissipate.

I think this is a wonderful analogy for control. When I relinquish control, when I fully expand and open, then miracles start to happen.

Control Inventory Profile

Always trying to remain in control of your life and the lives of others is a sign that you have deep fear at your core. If you don't deal with that fear, you will continue to try to control things, only to find that you cannot. Getting to the root of your control issues takes huge courage and deep inner integrity. You have to be willing to take an honest, heartfelt look at yourself. If you don't, you will likely find that fear runs and can ruin your life.

Take a few minutes to do this Control Inventory Profile. Doing so will give you greater clarity on just how much fear is running your life.

A Moment in Time

OMG! How delightful the synchronistic dance that Universal Creation orchestrates within our lives! I was on my way to the coffee shop this morning to start my writing routine, and I was called by a radio-show host. A week ago, I got an intuitive hit to call in. While I was not chosen, the producer spoke to me and ended up calling me back for another contest.

I did the contest, and I won! Do I usually spend my time responding to radio contests? No. In fact, I have probably responded to about six in my lifetime, and ironically (or not), I won three of them. Again, this is about listening to that inner voice. With this contest, when I called in, the phone rang about twenty times, and I was disconnected. Then for some crazy reason, I called back again, and they responded.

Another time I did a contest while living in Vancouver. I won the contest and got free promotion on my acting-coaching business. As a result, a talent agency in nearby Nanaimo contacted me, and I ended up getting a contract as an on-camera acting coach for the agency.

Similarly, with the call today, while talking to the radio hostess, I mentioned that I was on my way to a café to finish writing this book. She asked more about it, and then encouraged me to send her the details once the book was completed. More potential free promotion!

Go figure, friends. When that voice (which is strong, but which doesn't always make sense) whispers, say yes, listen, and act on it. You never know what this wonderfully creative Universe has in store.

To really benefit from this profile, you need to commit to being brutally honest with yourself. If you are not, it will be fruitless. With some of the questions, you may need to seek feedback from friends and family members who will be forthright.

For each of the questions below, take care to pause and ask your deepest self for the truth. Then choose the number that is most closely aligns to your situation (1 being "not at all" and 10 being "a great deal").

1. How often do feel you have to be the one to run the show at work?

1 — 2 — 3 — 4 — 5 — 6 — 7 — 8 — 9 — 10

2. How often do you have to be the one to run the show at home?

1 — 2 — 3 — 4 — 5 — 6 — 7 — 8 — 9 — 10

3. How upset do you get when things don't go your way?

1 — 2 — 3 — 4 — 5 — 6 — 7 — 8 — 9 — 10

4. Do others say that you have a need to control things?

1 — 2 — 3 — 4 — 5 — 6 — 7 — 8 — 9 — 10

5. Do people fear your response if their ideas differ from yours?

1 — 2 — 3 — 4 — 5 — 6 — 7 — 8 — 9 — 10

6. Do you get nervous in a car when others are driving?

1 — 2 — 3 — 4 — 5 — 6 — 7 — 8 — 9 — 10

7. How much do you restrain your children because you are afraid they will get hurt?

1 — 2 — 3 — 4 — 5 — 6 — 7 — 8 — 9 — 10

8. Are you obsessive, feeling that everything has to be just right?

1 — 2 — 3 — 4 — 5 — 6 — 7 — 8 — 9 — 10

9. Are you afraid of crowds, concerned that strangers could attack you?

1 — 2 — 3 — 4 — 5 — 6 — 7 — 8 — 9 — 10

10. Do you hold a tight rein around your partner, family members, and friends, fearing that they will get hurt or will hurt you?

1 — 2 — 3 — 4 — 5 — 6 — 7 — 8 — 9 — 10

If you scored between 76 and 100, you can do some work on your fears around control (or lack thereof). Acknowledge yourself for taking this first step. Doing so and following through on the suggestions in this book will help you feel safer and allow yourself to be led by the inherent flow of the Universe. Have compassion for yourself, and when you can, recognize and feel into your fears. Witness them as they arise, and then allow them to fully express themselves, without judgment or condemnation. The more you witness, the more clarity you will have and the more decluttering you will do.

If you scored between 51 and 75, you're working on it. Good for you. You still have a way to go, but you have taken steps towards facing your fears and alleviating your control issues. Try to take tiny, incremental steps. Say, for example, you find that you are fearful when you go into a crowd. Before you do so, take some deep breaths and allow yourself to fully experience your fear. Watch it, and note where it sits in your body. After allowing it to be fully expressed, go into the crowd, and repeat the mantra, "I am safe, and I am loved." Note any shifts in your experience.

If you scored between 26 and 50, you're doing some very good work. You are learning how to trust, love, and honor yourself. Continue to observe yourself when you start feeling out of control. If you feel the need to control, have a candid conversation with the part of yourself that is experiencing the fear. The more you can speak with that part of yourself without being reactive, the more you will gain clarity on whether your fears are warranted or based in untruths. Above all else, observe and have compassion towards yourself.

If you scored between 10 and 25, wow! You're there. You have alleviated many of your control issues. In general, you trust that you are being taken care of and that you need not try to control everything in your life. Allow yourself to appreciate the part of you that has taken a giant step towards decluttering your brain and creating space for deeper connection, greater ease, and expanded consciousness in your life.

Letting Go of Judgments around Control

This profile should give you a barometric reading of the power of control issues in your life. With this information, you can begin to take steps towards trusting yourself and having faith that all is moving in the direction that it should in your life. Once you lift some of your control issues, you will find yourself worrying a lot less and having a great deal more energy.

My Controlling Attitude

All right. I've done the profile and I admit it. I'm a recovering control freak! Sometimes we're so quick to see everybody else in our lives that way: My parents were control freaks. That friend of mine is a control freak. My ex-husband is a control freak. With deeper reflection, I started seeing how much I tried to control, and still do.

First and foremost, underneath control is fear. Trying to push away the attempts to control or trying to push away the fear does not help. It's a matter of having compassion for ourselves and feeling that it's OK to fear; it's OK to be a control freak.

Letting Go and Seeing a Rebirth

Although I received wonderful reviews for my solo theatrical production, *Causeless Joy* (formerly *Beauty, Bollywood, and Beyond*), in New York, LA, and Chicago, I was struggling with marketing it. When I look deeper, I have had some judgment and emotional blocks around self-promoting. My sense of lack and fears around selling seats was a real "opportunity" that I had several chances to overcome.

After many failed attempts at filling seats at national and local venues, I became very aware of my sense of hopelessness. Then one day, I was invited to a friend's house to play the game of Catalyst. In the game, we each focus on one particular issue that we would like clarity on, and I chose the issues around promoting my solo show. While I was not specifically guided to do so, when I got home that evening, I decided to let the show go. I gave up seeking new venues or trying to promote it. After so much angst, it felt good to let it go. I thought that perhaps it was time to move on. Maybe I was in a different place in my life, and perhaps a different show might be percolating in my subconscious. Either way, I was done, and the weightiness of my frustration and anger around it melted away.

Within two weeks, I got an email from the Sara-Solo Festival in Florida offering me performance dates at their upcoming event. The next day, I got another email from a local church minister, who had heard about me through a member of her congregation. She and I met for breakfast and quickly realized that we were kindred spirits. I booked a full month of weekend performances at her church. *Causeless Joy* was reborn.

Once I was able to pull away from my angst and anger, the toxic energy around it lifted from my psyche. My brain decluttered, creating an energetic vacuum that allowed room for other opportunities to arise.

Behind Apparent Arrogance Is Insecurity

Many times, we consciously or unconsciously try to take control of situations because of fear. I am constantly witnessing myself and the dramas I create around my control issues. For example, I noted in the past that if somebody else took a leadership role, I would respond with the inner notion that *I* should be leading, that *I* was better qualified. Then I asked myself what the truth was behind the discomfort and arrogance.

As I investigate, I see that it is fear. What is the fear voice inside of me saying? "Perhaps they are better than me. What if they are? What if they know more?" If I relinquish control, I worry that I may not be good enough, I may not be worthy, and I might be a failure. It comes back to that sense of self—who am I without the doing, without being the leader, without having control?

For parents, some of our greatest lessons come from our children, because often we cannot control what our children do. At some point, we have to relinquish control, and it can be scary.

Often these reactions aren't conscious. For me, the greatest lesson is to note in my body, my mind, and my heart if I'm feeling uncomfortable or anxious. At the workplace, I often get anxious, and I'll stop and think, "What's really going on here? I don't have control. I feel out of control." What is the deeper fear? The fear that I won't be successful, and if I'm not successful, I could be fired or laid off.

Choose Compassion over Judgment

Don't judge the aspect of yourself that wants control. Judging will exacerbate the problem. Again, as you have done in some of the previous exercises, take yourself back to being a child who's fearful and wants control. Acknowledge the fearful little person. Acknowledge the child, go within, and work with the fear. Then make a conscious choice to relinquish a little bit of control and see where the Universe guides you.

Exercise 21: Relinquishing Control

Here is an exercise in relinquishing control. Take a deep breath in, and as you do, go into your heart. See the heart feeling safe and secure. See it wide open and radiating white light. Feel the warmth of love emanating from that light filling your entire body, head to toe. Breathe out any anxiety or fears, witnessing your mind, and watching the thoughts as they come and go.

Now think of a situation in which you need to maintain control. Try and find the one that has the most charge for you and see it into your mind's eye. After you note it, take another deep breath. Check in with your body. Is there any tightness in certain areas? If so, simply notice where it rests in the body and observe it.

Now continue imagining the person or scene that you want to control. Watch the worst-case scenario unfold, and as it does, ask yourself, "Is this so bad?" If you observe yourself being fearful or trying to control the situation, stop.

Offer up that fear, that sense of control or lack thereof, to your Divine. As you do, see yourself as a tiny child. Tell yourself, "You're enough. You're enough just by being who you are. You don't need to shine or prove anything to anyone." See your Divine telling you, "You are enough. I see you and I have plans for you. Trust in me and know that you are safe. All is good." If you see the Creative Force as beyond human, sit with the knowing that all is in order as it should be.

Surrender and trust that when you relinquish control, good things will follow. Take a deep breath in, and when you feel ready, open your eyes.

The Folly in Trying to Control Others

How much do you judge others for being controlling? As I have previously stated, our outer world is a mirror reflection of our inner world. I often catch myself getting upset with others who are controlling. Why? Because I have issues within me about my own controlling tendencies.

I believe that as we struggle with control, our body's energy decreases, and ultimately our immune system can start to fail. Holding on to worry, control, and regret, telling yourself, "I should really relinquish control. I have to give it up," lowers your energy frequency. You can become very fatigued.

So have compassion. If you observe the critic in you saying, "You should know better," stop and breathe.

On the other hand, if you want to take control, then just do it. Don't beat yourself up.

One last point: it's wonderful to cultivate the witness-self. When you do, you are both in the drama and watching it at the same time. Why don't you giggle a little bit as you witness, noting, "Here I go again. There's the controller taking over." Play and find some humor in that drama. Think of yourselves as a little children in the schoolyard, playing those games and wanting control at a very young age, and then be with it. The more you're OK with your need to control, the more you will watch it dissipate. Ultimately, the more you develop a deeper relationship with the Universal Creator, the more you trust that all is well in your life. You let go and you let God.

Gratitude Begets More to Be Grateful For

Throughout this book, I have referred to the potency of gratitude. The more I express gratitude, the more I feel my heart exploding with delight. In fact, expressing gratitude is the fastest and most intense way of opening my heart.

As I have pointed out, recent studies have revealed that it is impossible for anyone to be depressed while experiencing gratitude. Knowing this, I often contemplate things that I am grateful for in my life when I find myself falling into discouragement or hopelessness.

I find that the expression of gratitude coincides with the "yes" shifting that I do in my head. As I start the "yes" process and imagine a "yes" day, my mind simultaneously scans for everything I am grateful for. The two move hand in hand and are a very mighty combination. You might try noting your energy prior to doing these practices and then pay attention to the shift thereafter. I don't think you will be disappointed. They both join forces to raise your consciousness, as well as your emotional and physical energy.

Wealth Reaches Deeper than Your Wallet

One of the greatest opportunities I have had towards raising my consciousness has been the work I have done around wealth. For decades, I thought that my wealth was only reflected in the size of my bank account. However, as of late, it has become crystal-clear that wealth incorporates so much more.

A couple of years ago, after leaving the corporate world, I took part-time jobs as a teacher to supplement my income. I was graced with an opportunity to work with children from a couple of months old through to eighteen years of age. If you remember how your class treated substitute teachers, you can imagine how tough it can be at times. That being said, I received so much grace from the experiences. With the younger children, I was able to tap into play and present-moment living alongside them. With the older students, I was given a glimpse of their world. They shared their fears and tears, their feelings of promise and hopelessness in a way that etched itself into my soul.

In response, I started several programs under the umbrella of "edutainment" productions, integrating emotional intelligence development with enjoyable and engaging initiatives. One program, Power Princesses and Superheroes, is growing at a record pace throughout preschools. Combining costume, magic, and storytelling, I recontextulize existing paradigms, teaching that princesses don't need to be saved and superhero strength can be rooted in kindness. Each time I get into my power princess or superheroine costume, I am filled with awe and gratitude. I feel privileged and humbled that I get to consciously play with the most lively, joyful beings I know. We laugh, we love, we tumble and fly around the room, ready each week for the next adventure.

I felt that the Universe had handed me a nugget of emotional gold, much more valuable than any gold found under the earth's surface. I had an opportunity to live heartily and fully in the moment with these children. They invited me into their precious, innocent world, where the awe of playing with colors and visiting the land of make-believe were all that mattered.

The real delight was that they felt my presence with them. Their hearts could feel my heart. Our hearts were melded into one delicious creative soup. I was the one who did the real learning, and I feel blessed to have had an opportunity to skip with them in their magical world.

Whether you are feeling stuck, or struggling with control issues, when you commit to living with inner integrity and have the desire to declutter the brain, finding gratitude for each and every step of the journey eases the path, and brings you a greater sense of well-being and a deeper connection to Source.

Step 8

Expect the Unexpected; Miracles Abound

The eighth and final step to decluttering your brain is to be expectant. When you expect the unexpected, miracles abound!

It's time to do your last profile. This is your Miracle Matrix Profile. It will give you perspective on just how in sync your life currently is.

Miracle Matrix Profile

Your life can be full of miracles, and the more you are aware of them, the more they will continue to manifest. This profile will shed light on how aware you are of the miracles that abound in your life. For each of the questions below, choose the number that most closely aligns with your thoughts and feelings (1 being "not at all" and 10 being "a great deal").

1. Are everyday miracles continuing to increase in your life?

1 — 2 — 3 — 4 — 5 — 6 — 7 — 8 — 9 — 10

2. Do you frequently get messages that you follow, and if you do so, do you find that you are pleasantly surprised?

1 — 2 — 3 — 4 — 5 — 6 — 7 — 8 — 9 — 10

3. Do you have friends whose lives shine with synchronicities as well?

1 — 2 — 3 — 4 — 5 — 6 — 7 — 8 — 9 — 10

4. Do you feel more and more joyful about simple things in life, like fall leaves, a tasty orange, or watching puppies play?

1 — 2 — 3 — 4 — 5 — 6 — 7 — 8 — 9 — 10

5. Do you experience deeper and deeper love for others and for yourself?

1 — 2 — 3 — 4 — 5 — 6 — 7 — 8 — 9 — 10

6. Do you find yourself analyzing the "why" of your feelings less, and allowing yourself more to move through them?

1 — 2 — 3 — 4 — 5 — 6 — 7 — 8 — 9 — 10

7. Are you less and less interested in gossiping and criticizing others?

1 — 2 — 3 — 4 — 5 — 6 — 7 — 8 — 9 — 10

8. Do you have increasing reverence for your surroundings, for example, taking better care of nature?

1 — 2 — 3 — 4 — 5 — 6 — 7 — 8 — 9 — 10

9. Do you find yourself being less critical and more appreciative of who you are?

1 — 2 — 3 — 4 — 5 — 6 — 7 — 8 — 9 — 10

10. Are you extremely committed to your self-care?

1 — 2 — 3 — 4 — 5 — 6 — 7 — 8 — 9 — 10

If you scored between 76 and 100, congratulations! Your life abounds with miracles, and you are aware of them. Look forward to greater synchronicities in your life. Be sure to surround yourself with like-minded individuals who delight in success and are committed to raising their consciousness and that of the planet. You are a model of conscious decluttering and will raise the energy and spirits of those who are graced with your presence.

If you scored between 51 and 75, you have come far on your journey towards decluttering your brain and welcoming more and more miracles in your life. As you continue to raise your consciousness, you will act on the hunches you receive, and experience more and more causeless joy in your life. Honor your commitment to your own personal growth and relish the joys that come your way.

If you scored between 26 and 50, you are on your way to experiencing more miracles in your life. While the voice of fear still clutters your brain, you will find that the more you take a witness stance and observe (instead of reacting to it), the less the voice will take command over you. Watch that voice, and commit to trusting in a benevolent, supportive Universe. The more you do this, the greater ease you will experience in your life and the more room you will have in your brain for creativity, innovation, joy, and ease.

If you scored between 10 and 25, you have many more opportunities for miracles to abound in your life. Start by saying the mantra, "I believe in my goodness, and I know that I deserve unconditional love to express itself in my life." Then focus on all of the goodness that you are and all of the kindness you have shared with others. Forgive yourself for the times when you acted against your best interests, and give yourself permission to move forward, knowing that you are loved and supported. Then anticipate miracles and celebrate them in gratitude when they occur.

What was your experience with the profile? Did it give you a broader perspective on your alignment with the miracles that abound in the world? The more aligned you are with what could be, the more open you are to be in a place of receiving.

Here's a new perspective that you might consider: The Universe does not measure miracles in terms of difficulty. The only measurement is in your beliefs. Manifesting a carrot is no different than manifesting a fourteen-karat gold diamond ring. The sense of effort involved is a reflection of our own beliefs.

Knowing That You Know

Now we're really at the point of getting out of our own way. The previous chapters were about removing the blocks, but at this point in the decluttering process, many of these have been removed. Now you can really start to shift and create a space for magic and miracles to manifest.

It's a delight to reach the stage in your life when you have a commitment, you have an absolute definitive—"I know this"—and start to cultivate it. Knowing that you really know is a wonderful place to be. The more you follow your heart, the more you fully take care of yourself. When you do so, you'll pay attention to the signs, large and small, and you'll start to go with the flow.

Have you ever experienced a deep and clear sense of absolutely knowing that something will transpire? This has happened to me many times, and when it does, it is magical. On a couple of occasions when I entered contests, I just knew I was going to win. At other times, although my logic told me otherwise, I illogically followed my heart guidance, and something wonderful and right happened in response.

There comes a time when you absolutely know that something is going to transpire; it's a feeling in your body. In my opinion, that is one of the central keys to manifesting in our lives. The million-dollar question is: "How do you cultivate it?"

A Moment in Time

As I sit here and write, I get a hit to listen to a song on my cell phone. The first one to appear is Michael Buble's "I Just Haven't Met You Yet." As I dance around the classroom, I feel my body fill with joy at the possibility of sharing my life of laughter and love with a partner. As I dance, I envision lightness and love between us, among my family members, and in the world in general. My day begins, and as the children enter the classroom, they feel it. The air is filled with a chorus of resounding yesses, and the energy is palpable. The joy explodes into delightful, connected possibilities for the hours ahead. Another magical day has begun.

Cultivating the Knowing

Forget about the *how*. Simply put it out to the Universe, and trust that you have been heard. If you think about it, how many times have you had a goal that you wanted to manifest in this world? You put it out there, you affirm, you visualize, you feel into it, and you think, "Now I have to think of how. Maybe I should do this or that." What happens to your energy? It starts to fall. What happens to your sense of hope? It starts to diminish. You talk your way out of it.

I can't tell you how many things have happened when I have emphatically said, "OK, Universe, this is going to happen. I don't know how, but I know that it will." The real delight is watching it unfold as the

Universe orchestrates incredibly synchronistic events. The trick is to unencumber yourself about the *how*. Forget about it.

Setting an Intention to Sell All

When I left Vancouver to move to Chicago, I put this decree out: "I can't lug this stuff across the country. I'd have had to pay for it all, with big problems at the border. Universe, this is what I want: I want to sell this apartment, along with every piece of furniture, painting, and knickknack. I want somebody to come in here, fall in love with it, and buy it all." Again, there was a strong energy, a deliberateness in my intention.

A neighbor on the floor below had a girlfriend, and when he heard I was moving out, he asked to show her around the place. Her response: "I want it all just the way it is, from every knickknack to every piece of furniture." How wonderful! My move was simplified, I made some extra money, and my confidence in my decorating ability was encouraged.

Appreciate and Watch the Synchronicities Grow!

As you experience these synchronicities more and more, the trick is to be truly grateful and appreciative. As you are, the experiences multiply. When I exercise, I have conversations with my body parts: "Heart, you're awesome. You're pounding like crazy here. Knees, I can't believe all the beating you have done for fifty-plus years. You're so strong and reliable. I love you." Then the heart and knees respond: "We love you too, Theresa. You take such good care of us, working out like this, and we appreciate your appreciation." Sounds crazy, but I believe that extending appreciation in whatever form, to whomever or whatever elevates our energy, raises our consciousness and effects greater positive change in our lives.

Appreciating the Pain

It can be hard to appreciate emotional or physical pain, but that's when you'll really see that you are growing.

At one point in Vancouver, I broke my commitment to make my living only doing creative endeavors. I started working for somebody in an office. They all seemed to be having so much fun, so I thought to myself, "I want to work with this guy."

I worked with him for several months. He ended up being a criminal and took a lot of money from people for some investment scheme. In the end, he owed me $5,000 in pay that I never saw.

If you make a decree, and it's a very strong one, you might want to stick to it. I ended up telling him that he was free to move on, that he didn't need to pay me. It was tough, but I believe that the angst I was feeling about his debt to me was affecting my physical and emotional well-being. It wasn't worth it. Perhaps someday that $5,000 will show up another time in my life, a time where I need it even more.

A Moment in Time

I put aside this Sunday morning to go to my local café and write this book. I was also scheduled to meet a fellow coaching friend whom I recently met covering a local Friends of Astrology event for the magazine. His name was Omari Martin, and we shared quite a potent exchange that penetrated our hearts and souls and left me in awe. He and I have both cultivated a strong trust in the still voice that guides us. We spent hours together, goal setting and supporting each other's career initiatives. While our personality-selves were present and engaged, the part of us that rests on the other side—our soul-selves—led the conversation. Our engagement was rooted more in the spirit than in the ego. Messages were coming to each of us a mile a minute. On this cool fall morning, images and dreams, insights and goals bounced from one to another, as if we were playing beach volleyball under the warm and wonderful Bahaman sun. The intensity of the spiritual interplay matched the heat of the tropical sands.

Exercise 22: Building Rapport with Your Higher Self

How do you get to the point of being emphatically sure of something? Practicing all of the tools I have shared about getting out of your own way starts to add up. You really have to trust your intuition. You need to listen and to actively respond to that knowing voice and watch for signs.

The trick is believing that the Universe is giving you messages and symbols. If you don't believe it, it's not going to happen. If you believe an angel card is just a bunch of baloney, it's going to be a bunch of baloney. If you don't believe a fortune cookie is going to have anything to say to you, it won't. That's part of the paradox: knowing that you really know is trusting.

Let me take you through an exercise to assist you with this step. Take some deep breaths in and out. See your heart and mind opening and expanding. Note any tightness in the body. Do not try to change it. Simply observe it.

Call upon Divine Guidance, whomever or whatever you consider it to be. Ask your Higher Self, "What do I need to know right now? What message do you want to share with me at this moment in time, that would serve me and the highest good of all?"

Just listen. It might be a symbol. It might be a picture or an image. It might be words. Simply listen.

If you don't have your message, trust again, knowing that you will get a message. It might come in your dreams. You might get a flash of an image later today or tomorrow, but trust that something is going to happen: something is going to come up for you.

Thank the Creative Source. Let it know that, while sometimes you forget, you know that you are always supported. You appreciate the support. Give thanks for the wonderful message and make every effort to act upon it.

When you feel ready, open your eyes. Take some time to write down the message that you received, and then commit to acting upon it in some way. It does not matter how big or small it is; just take a little action.

Sometimes you feel you have to do it all, and then you feel overwhelmed. But if you take a tiny step towards responding to that message, your higher guidance will be heard, and you will continue to receive more.

How Do You Know if the Guidance Supports You?

Does the thought of pursuing the initiative create a sense of enthusiasm or joy in you? If not, then perhaps it is not for you. Or, if it is based in negativity, then do not act upon it. You have to ensure that your intentions are pure and for the highest good of all. If you haven't done your emotional inventory on an issue, then be sure to do so. Be extremely honest with yourself and about your initiatives. Why are you doing this? Is there any sense of revenge, payback, or ill will toward another? If so, then you are listening to your ego or personality-self, and I encourage you to aim higher.

Writing the messages down can be very helpful. You can also share them with others, but make sure you're sharing them with somebody who's not a skeptic. Be sure it's somebody who's supportive.

There comes a time when you absolutely, emphatically know that something will transpire. The trick is methodically cultivating that extraordinary state of alignment. Again, the alignment means listening; it means honoring yourself. It means trusting there's something out there. It means paying attention and sending a very definite intention.

Overshadowing Your Shadow-Self

There's a lot of talk about dealing with the dark, mysterious shadow-self. Sometimes you can overshadow your shadow by asking yourself, "What's the shadow? Where am I going with it, and how am I living it?"

I discovered this paradox in my own life when I was taking an art class in Chicago. In this process, we were not to judge or critique the artwork in any competitive way.

I would go to the class, and I would set an intention. There were all kinds of materials for creating sculptures, paintings, or drawings. We would sit down and write about our process, then we would share our work with the group, or not. Either way, it was imperative that we took judgment out of the equation. It was forbidden.

One day the thought arose, "I have been avoiding my shadow-self for way too long. Theresa, stop avoiding. Courageously enter into the shadow zone." So I set an intention in the class to do a sculpture or a painting based on my shadow-self and let it get ugly and speak.

By the time the workshop ended, I had made a delightful aluminum-foil sculpture. There were little egg characters playing and picnicking. There was a big tree; in the middle of it was a pearl. When you looked at the sculpture, it reflected complete joy, total fun, and connection. I said to myself, "What is this? This is my shadow-self?"

I realized that I had always wrongfully labeled myself. As I previously mentioned, I saw my core self as grimy and ugly and dark. My shadow was, in fact, my divinity. In my commitment to seeking higher consciousness, the critic within me had been carrying this shadow-self on my sleeve. I was wearing the darkness and hid my light in the shadows. My shadow was actually my light. I had to own the light. That was the message that the sculpture brought my way.

There is a danger as we commit to decluttering the mess in our brains. We start to focus on the mess, and not on what is clean, pure, and good. If you were cleaning out your library or your wardrobe, if you only saw the items you no longer wanted, you would miss the magnificent items that you already have. We forget that we are divine, pure souls. Instead, we focus on what's not right, where we need to work, and where we believe ourselves to be dark. In my case, when I finally had the courage to face my shadow-self, I saw the light of who I am. You may find that same radiant light that shines within you as well!

Exercise 23: Casting a Light on the Shadow

I am going to take you through a short process to help you uncover your shadow.

Commit to being very open. Close your eyes and take a deep breath in. See your heart expanding and your mind opening. Relaxing your body, melt any tension, call in divine protection, and ask for the highest good.

Now ask your shadow to reveal itself to you. Keep breathing deep breaths in and out. Allow yourself to be present. See if an image or words arise. Whatever comes up from you, allow it and listen.

Then ask your shadow if it has a message for you. Take note of that message. Ideally, take some time to write it down. If you are unclear, ask for additional guidance. Once you feel that the dialogue is complete, then thank your shadow: "You're a part of me. Every part of me is Divine, so thank you. Thank you for speaking and connecting with me. Thank you for showing yourself and having the courage to come out and play. Thank you, shadow."

When you feel ready, open your eyes.

If you've received a symbol, you can ask, "What does this symbol mean?" Allow it to percolate inside you, and you'll start getting messages. Your shadow may surprise you, or it may not. Whatever the outcome, it will raise your inner awareness and consequently your consciousness.

Focusing on Not Being Focused

We can be very hard on ourselves. Often we focus on the fact that we're not focusing. We have to be careful, because if we keep focusing on this, what are we going to manifest? We'll never be focused.

People might respond, "That seems awfully simple." It *is* simple, although following through on it isn't always easy. When you say, "I'm really not good at getting up in the morning," you're not going to be good at getting up in the morning. Or if you say, "I'm really not very good at writing down my goals and following through on them," you won't do it. Start speaking in the positive, and catch yourself when you're saying things that are negative and derogatory.

Another big part of focusing is trusting that you are guided, and that you don't have to do it all. As I've said in the past, forget about the *how*.

You can set an intention or say a prayer: "I really want this, Universe. I don't know how. I'm going to trust that you're going to provide me the *how*." After my car awakening experience, I always request ease and joy in the experience. Being specific produces clarity around your desires, which can only serve to benefit you.

Focusing on your desires can be fun! When I was going through my divorce, I spent every day journaling. Journaling is more than just intending or seeing or wishing an experience. It's feeling it fully with all of our senses. So every day for at least six months, I would write in my journal. As I was writing, I would start to giggle. I would feel the delight in every bone of my being.

Within a year of journaling, a real-estate agent friend found a condo for me. It was everything I dreamed of. I furnished it in the exact way I wanted to, and it manifested literally, right down to the fireplace with the on/off switch, the big bedroom full of windows, and the big kitchen with granite countertops. It was gorgeous. It came from the delight that was bubbling inside me as I wrote in my journal. I could feel it with every ounce of my being. By doing that, I got out of my own way, and allowed things to take shape, from my subconscious and into my life.

Although this may sound far-fetched, everything has energy. Even a chair holds the energy of the people who have been sitting in it. You can take this as literally or as loosely as you want.

Creating a Vision Board

Another method is creating a vision board. It's fun to do, especially if you have kids. Get a bunch of magazines, or go on the Internet, and find pictures of things you really want—homes, pools, vacation sites. Put them on a board, arranging them thematically.

I would encourage you to do a dream board as well. This year I created a little dream adventure box, full of pictures and symbols. I have worked with a wonderful healer, Lisa Schwartz, in Chicago, who does intention dolls. You can create these dolls and fill them with symbolic intentions too. In whatever form you want, set into motion your desires through visuals, words, smells—whatever senses are calling out to you.

Doing this kind of exercise can be creative and fun. When you focus on what you really want, the things you focus on usually start to manifest quite quickly.

When Things Don't Manifest as Planned

Sometimes we want our desires to manifest immediately, but sometimes they don't. Why? It could be that, in the whole scheme of our lives, manifesting them at the time, place, and in the situation that we think is for our highest good, is not.

This is where faith comes in. We have to trust that things will work out as they should, when they should. Moreover, we may still have blocks to overcome. You will likely find that, as you remove the blocks by consciously observing them and asking questions of them, they will weaken. In time, as you focus on what you want and start seeing and feeling those images on a regular basis, that will overshadow and overtake negative impulses. The energy becomes so high that it reaches a breaking point, at which time the Universe hears you and responds accordingly.

When You Know, You Need Not Prove

This brings up another point. When you get to a place of knowing, especially around your spirituality, you don't have to prove it to anyone. You don't have to convince or prove anything to anyone.

You know in your heart that which you know, and if others are ready and curious, they will come to you.

At the audio company, I was considered the woo-woo lady who did all the spiritual producing. Even in a place like that, people were very skeptical. Nonetheless, many would quietly come into my office and tell me stories about their psychic experiences, or they'd say, "I have an ache here. Do you think you could do some energy work with it?"

Check in with yourself. If you feel a sense of, "I have to tell everybody and convince everybody about this," your desire to share can come from enthusiasm—"I want to share this spiritual connection that I have with the world"—and you can honor that enthusiasm. However, I believe that enlightened masters like Christ or the Buddha got to the place where they wanted to help heal the world, but they did not need to prove their authenticity. They got to a place where they frankly didn't care. They were not out to prove anything to anyone, because they had cultivated that strong inner knowing.

So you might check in with yourself. Where are you in that respect? Do you feel a need to help others see life from your perspective or belief system, or are you comfortable with the path they have chosen? Allow yourself to focus on that which serves your highest good, your highest knowing. In doing so, allow and acknowledge others for their different beliefs and perspectives. Doing so strengthens your inner knowing and provides you with the flexibility to allow others the same courtesy.

The Gift of Silence and Stillness

For many years, I knew that meditation would be really good for me. For several decades, the thought kept arising, "I really should meditate." I know it would change my life forever. I knew that my response to stressors would decrease and that my health and well-being would greatly improve. Nonetheless, I never had the patience to sit in silence, even for a couple of minutes. I spent years and years avoiding it at all costs.

What was I so afraid of? Perhaps I wanted to maintain my identity with the busyness of my life. Perhaps I was afraid to face who and what I am at my core.

Finally, I took the vipassana intensive that I mentioned previously. Sitting and observing the mind from 4:00 a.m. to 8:00 p.m. each day was a challenge. What I found most difficult was sitting in silence with the clutter in my brain and the constant churning of the crazy monkey mind. It was fascinating, watching it flitter about. It was also grueling for me to remain focused and present at times.

Yet the vipassana intensive was a saving grace. Incredibly, I found that after sitting an average of twelve hours each day for ten days, sitting for thirty minutes to one hour each day became much easier.

Now when I sit in silence, I can feel into my body. I feel the energy moving through it, and I am able to move in and out of the witness state.

Focusing on the Quiet and Wise Voice Within

For many years, I would get a lot of inklings, and I'd ignore them. You've probably had this experience, where you'll get a little voice in your head saying, "You really shouldn't do that." Then you do it and you say, "I knew it. This little voice said not to do it. Why don't I listen to that little voice?"

I've missed so many opportunities in my life. I would say, "There it is again. Darn it all, why do I do this? I know otherwise." Sometimes the guidance makes no logical sense whatsoever. But finally, you say to yourself, "How many times do I have to be hit over the head to know that this is a sign? I need to listen."

If you start focusing on what you haven't focused on—"What am I not listening to?"—you will start to cultivate the listener-self.

Some people say that miracles can become commonplace. They never have for me, and I don't know if they ever will. That's a good thing. It's so delightful to be bubbling with enthusiasm, joy, and gratitude when they manifest. The miracles are always there; they're sitting in waiting. Gratitude raises our energy frequency to align with them. Gratitude, like forgiveness, is a massive gift to yourself.

When I've believed that the Universe is working with me, things fall into place easily and effortlessly. I think everyone's looking for more ease in their lives.

So intend it and trust that your message is heard, and that the Universe is collusive and responding.

Exercise 24: Experiencing the Perfect Day

Let's do an exercise with dream creating.

Get quiet again. Do some deep breathing; connect with your body. Connect with *now*. Feel into your body. Open your open heart. Open your mind.

Now focus with unyielding commitment on your perfect day. You're lying in bed. Where are you living? Are you by mountains or by the ocean? Are you in a little cottage or a huge mansion? Are you by yourself, or do you have a sweet love beside you? What does your perfect morning look like?

You stretch. You get out of your bed. What does your body look like? What does your health feel like? What smells are coming in? The salt of the sea? The pines in the mountains?

As you stretch your body, how does it feel? You look in the mirror. It's a perfect day. You feel wonderful. What do you see? You go into the closet. It might be a huge walk-in, or a tiny one in a cottage. Pick out clothing. What feels good?

It's time for breakfast. Does your sweetheart make you breakfast? Do you have a special cook who provides you with healthy meals?

You go downstairs. What does your home look like? You look out the window. What do you see? Are there children laughing and chattering? Is it quiet? Do you hear waves on the shore? Are you overlooking a beautiful lake or stream? Are you in a tree house or on the ground? What part of the world do you live in? Are you in America? Europe? Africa?

It's a perfect day, and you are grateful. Everything is falling into place on this perfect day.

Do you go to work? Do you stay home? Are you being rewarded or honored for being outstanding in a certain field? Are you doing charity work?

What do your friends look like? Feel into the delight of sharing and laughing with those friends. What kind of connection do you have with them? Are you having dinner together somewhere?

Your soul is feeling expanded and appreciative. What is your connection to the Divine or Universal Source? Are you experiencing synchronicities in your life that delight you?

Going through the day, what do you do first thing in the morning? Do you take a walk along the beach? Do you go out and do a couple of ski runs? How do you feel? Does your body feel weightless, buzzing with energy, vitality, health?

How do you fill your afternoon? Lunch with friends? Dancing lessons? In the evening, do you go to the theater? To dinner?

Focus on your perfect day. Feel into it. Smell the smells. If you're eating, what favorite foods are you eating? Taste the tastes.

If you go outside, is it hot? Is it cool? Is there a slight breeze? Feel it against your cheek. Are your feet bare, or are they in comfy slippers or wonderful shoes?

Whom are you connecting with? Whom are you playing with? Whom are you laughing with? How do you feel about yourself on your perfect day? See how divine you are; see your creativity manifesting in the world in wondrous ways; see the work you've done on yourself healing thousands of others. You are modeling joy and connectedness for them. You are changing the world.

When you feel ready, see the day coming to an end. You're back in your cozy bed. Maybe there's a fireplace in the bedroom. Maybe you're with a loved one. Maybe you're joyful on your own. Whatever that looks like, thank the Universe. Know that you've cocreated the day.

You've put a call out to the Universe about this perfect day. That call can transmit and transmute powerful energy. When you feel ready, open your eyes.

You energize what you focus on. Setting a strong intention, being unwavering, and holding steadfastly to it is the most powerful thing you can do to manifest. I encourage you to go through this exercise and every day start feeling, with all of your senses, into what you want in your life. Then feel gratitude. Trust that you're putting that energy out there, and it's being heard.

Doing What You Love Loves You
As you progress in decluttering your brain, cultivating the witness-self, and listening in the present moment

in your life, you start to realize that what you love really loves you. It wants you to succeed and wants to come to you. In fact, it's just waiting. This is a wondrous place to be.

Most of us have been brought up with a belief system saying that we have to work hard 9:00 to 5:00—or in today's world, ten- or twelve-hour days—so that we can eventually own our own home and retire comfortably. If we believe this, our lives will unfold as such. If that's what you love—or at any rate if that's what you tell yourself you need to do—that's what you're going to experience.

Living for Tomorrow: Another Brain Trap

Have you noted how much many of us live for tomorrow? "I'm going to work hard at a job I hate for twelve hours a day, for forty years of my life, so when I'm older and getting tired (and can't travel the way I want to or even climb the stairs comfortably), then I'll get a big house, start traveling, and have all my plans come to fruition."

You have to find balance. If you believe you have to suffer and do a job you hate in order to succeed in life, you will create this. But you don't have to.

I've been graced in being able to do what I want in life. I became an actress, and I loved it. I traveled the world, and I loved it. Then I got the producing job, and I loved that as well. Later I took a job as a corporate trainer. I was able to travel throughout the country, honing my skills as a motivational speaker and connecting profoundly with fellow staff members.

Even some of the jobs I've taken that have been bridges rather than career paths have given me such gifts. After leaving the production company, I did freelance work for several years, which was fun. Then I thought, "I'm going to try to get some steady income and benefits." The job I took got me through so many things, and it also honed some skills.

When I did the exercise about my perfect day and perfect life, it was about traveling and showing my daughter a big, beautiful world. Again, it's that absolute, definitive knowing. I'm not doubting it, and in fact it's already coming. Doing what you love will come to you, but you have to have faith, and it's also important to be really clear.

Doing what you love, seeing what you love, being with those you love will come to you. The more you do this work, the more you get out of your own way. As we've done with the exercises here, you continue to cleanse your mind and clear out the clutter. You gain a sense of knowing, and in time, you find yourself delighted and in anticipation, thinking, "It's coming. I know it's coming. I can't wait to see how," because you are not worrying about the *how*.

Sometimes compromise can play a role, as long as you don't get lost in it. We have to be careful about compromising, because if we live life completely as compromised and really don't believe that we can have what we want, that is what we will experience. If a job is a bridge, and if we're still holding on to our dreams and working towards what we really want, that's fine. I've had two jobs that I saw as bridges, and they were perfect at the time. They weren't what I loved to do, but they were stepping-stones.

When I'm in the career bridges, I know that they are not going to last too long: "Thank you, Universe. You provided me what I need right now. I need the insurance, and assurance. I need to tend to the bank account."

Knowing What You Want

Some people may say they don't really know what they love or want to do in life. But I worked with an author who said that everyone knows what they want. They just may not be willing or ready to go there.

One trick is to go back into your childhood and find out what you had fun doing then. Reflect on what you loved to play or pretend. Write out what you love to do, what really inspires you and creates passion in you. Then, from that, start writing details. How can you package that into a career? How can you monetize these interests? Again, don't spend too much time focusing on how. Focus more on creating the vision of what you really want.

"I'm writing, and I'm eating wonderful food. How can that combine? OK, Universe, give me some answers here. What do we see? A travel writer. Let's go to the local newspaper. Can I start a column about my travels? It'd be fun."

It's about saying to yourself, "I'm going to stop at nothing to make this happen." It often involves stepping out of your comfort zone. You might have to improve the quality of what you do to the point that you're feeling satisfied with it. If you have never been a writer, for example, you might have to take some courses.

You can also be creative in your approach. Find different ways. For myself, I've had thousands of different inventions come into my mind, but I'd say, "I don't know how to do that," or, "I have no idea how to get a patent."

As ideas come up, I would encourage you to do something about them, even if it's putting them out there on social media. It's amazing what people can do. You can do five minutes on an idea on social media, get lots of watchers, and there's your new career. Technology being what it is, the world today is very much about immediate action and immediate response.

Take tiny baby steps, as I did at the audio company. It was so clear to me that I needed to be there, and I was so committed, that I said, "Don't pay me. I don't care." Before I knew it, I was getting paid and I was head over heels in love with the career move that I had made.

If you dream of having your own tea shop, what baby step can you take to start on that path? Perhaps you could approach a local golf course in the off-season and organize one tea on a Sunday when they are closed. Invite your friends and see what happens.

The step doesn't have to be big. The important thing is to proclaim: "OK, Universe, I really want this, and I don't know how. I have no idea, but you're going to start showing the way, and little things are going to start to happen—synchronicities. I'm waiting, and I'm looking forward to it."

Exercise 25: Expressing Your Gratitude

Let's do an exercise on gratitude.

Take a deep breath in, closing your eyes, relaxing into your seat, opening your heart, opening your mind, observing and letting go of any tension in the body.

If you don't know what you want to do, go to your ten-year-old self and ask, "What do I want to do in my life? What do I love? What do I have a passion for? What brings me joy? Is it travel, is it decorating, is it organizing? Is it children, is it seniors? What do I really love?"

If you don't get an answer, trust in that, and have the faith that something will come to you soon. If you get an answer, imagine yourself doing what you really love. You're smiling; you are enjoying it. It's very successful, it's easy, and it's effortless. The right people and the right opportunities are making their way to you. Money is flowing into your bank accounts. You can say:

"I am making so much. I am so appreciated. People are telling me how much what I'm doing is affecting their lives. There is peace and contentment. If I want to, I have lots of free time to relax, enjoy, and travel. If I want, I have people working for me. They love what they do. They feel supported. They love coming into work every day to be with me.

"Creative ideas are flourishing, and my business is growing. As it grows, I get the support that I need. The right people come into play at the right time. The work environment is easy, fun, and respectful. It flows. There is joy. There is a sense of oneness, a sense of sharing, encouragement, laughter, ease, and honoring. I am doing what I really love.

"Everything is falling into place. It is constantly growing, shifting, and changing. I feel supported. I feel such gratitude. Thank you to all for the help that has come my way.

"At the end of each day, I am energized, I am at peace, and I am so grateful that I'm aligned with my soul's desire. And so it is."

Now you can open your eyes.

If you fall off the wagon and need to reinspire yourself, you can go back to this exercise and take little baby steps, whatever they might be. Trust that the Universe has your back, that it is guiding and fully supporting you.

If you have doubts that you're supported, ask the Universe, "Please show me. Show me how you support me. Reveal yourself to me." Then watch and wait and learn, and it will show itself.

A Lesson in Faith from a Hummingbird

I love hummingbirds. In the Andean shamanic tradition, they represent the ancestor of the north. One summer I was at my sister's house, and a hummingbird got stuck in her garage. We opened the doors to allow it to leave, but when we returned later that day, it was dead. I was devastated.

A year later, my neighbors had a hummingbird in their garage and they called me over. I asked for a ladder, but the husband would not get me one. "There's nothing you can do," he said.

"Yeah, there is," I said. My love for hummingbirds goes very deep. I've studied and practiced Andean Shamanism. Many times I have called out to them and welcomed their presence in ceremony. I note how they defy logic, with the mind-boggling speed of their wings, along with a heart rate that can reach as high as 1,260 beats per minute.

I grabbed a ladder, and I got a plate of water and sugar. I put my hand out to the hummingbird. I was totally present and felt deep, soulful love for that bird, and I know that it felt that love. It didn't go near the plate of sugar water. It landed directly on my hand, and it allowed me to take it out of the garage. I never wrapped my fingers around its tiny body. It perched quietly upon my open palm and graced me with its mysterious and mystical presence.

Like the hummingbird, we are each unique miracles of Creation. Our souls are connected to the Divine, and the Divine feels the love. Like the silent and still winged messenger, all we need do is completely trust. When you do, like my empty, anticipating palm, your energy is wide open. Doing what you love will easily and effortlessly come to you, just as that hummingbird came to me.

A Moment in Time

As I sit here in the café, looking out the window, I am observing the plethora of colors that dance around me in the fall breeze—above and below, weaving about in the wind. I breathe deeply as I ingest the glory of the color parade all around me, as the trees transition from the sweet sweat of summer into their spectacular autumn coats.

Tears of joy and gratitude fill my eyes as I note their perfection. And yet I see the individual leaves. Each has its own blackened pockmarks. Some have massive holes. Others are weathered and worn, their edges browning, bending, and dry. Yet, with each flaw present and visible, in its entirety the tree is absolute perfection. As each trunk stretches towards the heavens, each hue fades one into another. I am overwhelmed with the magnificent pallet that sweet Mother Earth uses to paint each tree—individual and glorious.

As I allow my mind to melt into the colors of the trees, I see how we are each a part of creation's perfection—each with our delightful and deliberate pockmarks, fully whole and fully human!

Love speaks to your soul and beckons you to follow it. All you need to do is surrender and trust it. Like that beautiful bird, all you love will come to you. The Universe feels it, knows it, and honors it.

A wonderful channeler I've worked with had a delightful insight about abundance and success. She said, "What if you deserve winning just by being on this earth? What if it's enough just to be here so that all the abundance you want, all the creativity you want to manifest in your life comes to you? It's not because you've done anything to be rewarded for. It's not like you've karmically worked really hard and therefore earned it. Just by being on this earth, being courageous enough to be a soul on this earth at this time, is all you need for everything you've ever dreamed of. You don't have to work hard. You don't have to suffer to be a winner. You just have to appreciate the fact that you chose to be here at this time, and that's enough."

Conclusion

There Are No Accidents

Now that you have invested enough time in yourself to journey through this book and do the profiles and experiential exercises, you may have a different perspective on your mind. Is it yours, or is it part of the thoughtmosphere? Therein lies the question, or does it?

What if the thoughts you catch from the thoughtmosphere have been magnetically drawn to you by your judgments? What if they have arrived into your brain for the sole purpose of allowing you to witness them, witness your inner critic, and then allow them to go where they will?

When I was very young, I got a clear message that my life's work is to heal the cruel critic within me, and in doing so, help others to heal theirs. At about the age of seven, I had a vision in a dream. I still remember the vision as if it were yesterday. Christ was sitting beside me, on a front porch step. At the time, I was struggling with my idea of a man who died for my sins (my shames, my darkness). A man who had a pejorative Father, both of whom were keeping tabs on my "good" behaviors and my "sinful" ones.

I believe that the dream was more than a passing fantasy. Just as my Nana came to me in a dream after her death, I believe that Jesus Christ was in fact sitting with me on that porch step. He looked deep into my eyes, and like Nana, sent me the most liberating and compassionate love. He was my big brother, and in seeing him that way, I have forever been changed.

The next time a thought enters your brain, one that you do not like, sit with it. Engage with it, and do so without judgment. Play with the fact that it is not yours, but a gift from this benevolent Universe. It is showing you where you are lacking love for yourself, where you are pushing yourself away from the love that always surrounds you.

I find myself in a constant dance with the push and pull of love and criticism. Here is an emergency repair kit that you can use when you find your energy falling and your sense of awe in your life depleted. Take three minutes to try one of the suggestions, noting your energy level both before you take the step and afterwards. All you need is the desire to float above your brain's clutter. The music, the delight, and the joys that you expose yourself to thereafter will do the rest.

Emergency Energetic Lift Kit

Sing and dance. Find a quiet place where you can be alone. Then go to YouTube, and type "inspiring music" in the search box. There are several mixes that are filled with contemporary music whose messages are encouraging. I dance to them and shake out any listlessness and negativity.

Spend time with children, puppies, kittens, and others who fill your heart with joy. If you can't physically visit with them, then look at videos of them on your cell phone or computer for a few minutes.

Take mininaps when you have a chance throughout your day. I will often go to my car when I have a couple of minutes, set my phone alarm and close my eyes for a catnap. I find that fifteen or twenty minutes is all I need to replenish my energy.

Compliment a stranger. I often walk up to others when the spirit moves me, and I tell them that I love their outfit, or that they have wonderful energy. If, for example, you are treated really well by a customer service rep, ask to speak to their manager so that you can commend them. Then note your energy and how you feel when you do this.

Take a couple of minutes to connect with nature. If you can, walk on the grass in bare feet, or visit a playground and try to touch the clouds on a swing. Allow yourself to be a child again for a few minutes.

Bless all involved when you eat. If you are eating a doughnut, do so without self-condemnation. Visualize all those who were involved with the creation of the food from start to finish, and thank each of them for their contributions.

Take a gratitude break. When you're feeling down, visualize all that you are grateful for in your life. If you feel extremely discouraged, just focus on one thing that you appreciate. It could be as simple as the scent of an orange.

Practice one minute of the Say Yes process. Take sixty seconds to reset your brain by focusing on the goodness that has come and will come your way, and keep saying yes, seeing your heart and mind opening as your energy rises.

Dip your face, feet, or hands in water. Take a few seconds to immerse some part of your body into water. Imagine all of the negativity going to that part, and see the water cleansing and clearing it. Feel into experiencing the refreshing water as it revitalizes you.

Give someone a sixteen-second hug. Studies have shown the great power of a good hug. However, most of us let go too soon. When you allow yourself to embrace another for at least sixteen seconds, there is a emotional and physical release that can shift negativity and energize both you and your co-hugger.

About the Author

Theresa Puskar is a highly skilled transformation leader, inspirational communicator and author. She has written over 50 motivational books and study guides, she has also authored seven children's books and a critically acclaimed solo stage production, *Causeless Joy*. The founder of *Edu-Tainment Productions*, she is an outstanding and versatile entertainer, weaving profound and often hilarious storytelling into all that she does. Known for her authenticity and unique ability to stir the hearts and minds of those with whom she engages, her refreshing and heartfelt *"tell it like it is"* approach to edu-taining supports greater compassion, consciousness and joy among her audiences.

CPSIA information can be obtained
at www.ICGtesting.com
Printed in the USA
JSHW042018050320
4606JS00003B/3

9 781722 502669